REFLECTING
the
GLORY

REFLECTING

the

GLORY

Tom

BIBLE READINGS AND REFLECTIONS

WRIGHT

FOR EVERY DAY IN LENT

 The Bible Reading Fellowship
OPENING THE BIBLE

Text copyright © 1997 Tom Wright

Published by
The Bible Reading Fellowship
Peter's Way, Sandy Lane West
Oxford, OX4 5HG
ISBN 0 7459 3556 7

First edition 1998

10 9 8 7 6 5 4 3 2 1 0

A catalogue record for this book
is available from the British Library

Printed and bound in Great Britain
by Caledonian Book Manufacturing International, Glasgow

Preface

This little book was the brainchild of the Reverend Shelagh Brown. She persuaded me to fit it into my busy schedule, and came in person to Lichfield with a tape recorder to coax out of me my reflections on some of the most exciting passages in the New Testament.

The plan was that Shelagh would then turn my taped ramblings into prose, submit it to me for further editing, and polish up a finished product. Alas, as many will know, she died tragically on 29 June 1997. At that stage, she had simply transcribed what I had said, but had not begun the editing process.

I am enormously grateful to the staff at The Bible Reading Fellowship, particularly Richard Fisher and Naomi Starkey, for coming to the rescue. Together we have turned the disjointed sentences into something more like English, and have produced a book which, I think, is not too far from what Shelagh herself would have wanted to see. Equally importantly, I hope the book has the effect Shelagh wanted—the effect, indeed, to which she devoted her very considerable energy in the last years of her life: that those who read it will come to a deeper, richer understanding and love of scripture, and, more importantly still, of the God revealed in Jesus, and supremely in his death and resurrection. I am honoured to be able to dedicate this book to Shelagh's memory, with thanks to God for her faith, joy, courage, and witness.

Tom Wright

October 1997

INTRODUCTION

At the heart of Christianity stands a particular claim: the one we call 'God' is known in and through Jesus of Nazareth.

That may be hard to swallow for those who do not profess Christianity. But even those of us who are believers find it difficult, because we know the stories of Jesus both too well and not well enough. 'Oh yes,' we think, 'I know this one'; and turn, say, the parable of the prodigal son into a simple lesson about the love of God. We generalize it: 'Yes,' we think, 'of course God loves us.' But we fail to realize the peculiar dynamic, the intensity and the drama of the parable. In fact, we constantly need to go back and remind our- selves who Jesus actually was, what he was actually like, and what the particular emphases of his parables actually were.

One of the reasons why we fight shy of doing this is that the more we make Jesus a believable first-century Jew the harder it is to see what he has to say to us today, either about God or about ourselves. We aren't first-century Jews. We haven't been invaded by a Roman army. We are not asking questions about paying tribute to Caesar. We often reduce the message of Jesus to a timeless, abstract statement of generalized truths, which we carry around with us and which are, frankly, boring. And then those of us who are theologians and teachers assume we have something called 'truth' in our back pocket, which we produce and shove down people's throats.

In fact, the truth about God being seen in Jesus is not like that at all. Truth is more like health. A doctor doesn't keep 'health' in his or her back pocket simply to throw at people. A doctor can work to create conditions for health and reduce the possibilities of illness. But ultimately health is a strange, mysterious thing that is part of God's gift of life. It is just the same with truth. The truth as it is in Jesus is personal truth, and Christians are not only summoned to *see* God in Jesus but also to *know* God in Jesus. Ultimately, we must learn to *love* God in Jesus.

You can't love an abstraction. You can't even love the idea of love. You can only truly love a person. The deepest, richest meaning of love must be personal love. The relevance of knowing God in Jesus is that when we love God in Jesus we discover how that love, that personal love, is given to us in order that it may be given through us. This is the point at which Christians, from the very beginning, have spoken of the Holy Spirit: the Spirit is the one who first enables us to love Jesus and then, in an extraordinary way, becomes the presence of Jesus in us, enabling us to love one another and shine the light of God's love into the world.

We can now understand how it is that the more we find out about Jesus, and particularly about his death and resurrection, precisely in their historical aspects, the more we are then energized by the Spirit to reveal God's love to the world. For me, the clearest statement of this is in John chapter 20. Jesus breathes on the disciples, and says to them, 'As the Father has sent me, so I send you. Receive the Holy Spirit.' Suddenly we see the whole vista of what God did in Jesus, through his healings and his suffering, through his parables, his celebrations, and ultimately his agony. And, with that, we discover that the story of Jesus' ministry is not only the story of what he did in history, but encompasses also the vocation that comes to us in the present: that we should be, in the power of the Spirit, the presence of Jesus for the whole world. This discovery brings us the most remarkable joy and the most remarkable sorrow. This is our vocation: to take up our cross, and be Jesus for the whole world, living with the joy and the sorrow woven into the pattern of our days.

In the light of all this, we begin our Lent readings with one of the most deeply personal and profoundly felt passages in the whole New Testament. It is a passage where Paul speaks of getting to the end of his tether and beyond. In 2 Corinthians 1:8 he speaks of being so unbearably crushed that he despaired of life itself. Part of the weight that was crushing him was the fact that the Corinthian church, with whom he had lived and worked for quite a long time, was casually rejecting him. In the passage we shall be studying for the first two weeks or so of Lent, he is writing to say that the pain he has received, and the puzzles, failings and difficulties he is enduring because of their rejection, are not signs that he has failed as an apostle. They are, in fact, the signs of a true apostle, bearing in his body the dying of Jesus as well as the life of Jesus. Accordingly, the whole middle section of 2 Corinthians (chs. 3–6) examines what it means to have the love and faithfulness of God in Jesus worked out by the Spirit in Christian ministry.

We shall then look at several other passages—from Paul, from the first letter of Peter, and from Revelation—in which this whole idea is worked out in an almost kaleidoscopic way. The different writers explore, in various ways, what it means to have the suffering and the glory of Christ incarnate in their lives through the Spirit, enabling them to be the people of God for the world.

We then take a deep breath and launch into the Gospel of John. The passages we shall study will take us through Good Friday, right up to Holy Saturday. At first we explore selected passages that highlight who Jesus is in the purpose of God: he is the one in whom the glory of God is revealed, who constantly challenges people to see God's glory in him and then to become, themselves, the bearers and vessels of that glory. Of course, throughout the first twelve chapters of John's Gospel, from which these selections are taken, not even the disciples, let alone the other onlookers, understand what's going on.

Then, in the last two weeks of Lent, from Passion Sunday to Palm Sunday, and through Holy Week to its final Saturday, we shall look at the so-called 'farewell discourses', John 13–17. We shall see Jesus gathering together the threads of all that he has done, and saying to his closest followers (the eleven who remain after Judas has gone out into the night), 'This is what has been going on in my work; and this is how it will be now for you.' Everything is gathered together into the remarkable prayer, sometimes known as the 'great high-priestly prayer', of John 17. There, Jesus prays for the church, and for the widening company of those who will come to believe in him through what the Eleven will do. We shall be looking at this prayer while, in the cycle of Lent, we are passing through the last three days: Maundy Thursday, where Jesus both prays the prayer and also lives it in his last supper with his followers; Good Friday, where he is acting as the great high priest, and doing that to which the prayer is pointing; and Holy Saturday, reflecting on the stillness, the extraordinary long breath before Easter Day, and contemplating Jesus as he goes to the lowest point of human experience on behalf of the world.

From Easter Sunday, for the first seven days of Eastertide, we turn to one of the most spectacular chapters in the New Testament.

1 Corinthians 15 is the first written exposition of the resurrection and all that it meant. There, in a great sustained argument, Paul explains what actually happened, what it means, and, in particular, where Christians belong on the new map that God has just drawn, the map of Easter life.

Throughout this Lent, then, we shall be looking at the dying and rising of Jesus, both as the final revelation of the glory of God, and as the blueprint for the vocation that is now given to God's people through the Spirit. This will be a challenging journey but, I hope, a richly rewarding one.

WEEK 1 (ASH WEDNESDAY)

2 CORINTHIANS 2:14–17

But thanks be to God, who in Christ always leads us in triumphal procession, and through us spreads in every place the fragrance that comes from knowing him. For we are the aroma of Christ to God among those who are being saved and among those who are perishing; to the one a fragrance from death to death, to the other a fragrance from life to life. Who is sufficient for these things? For we are not peddlers of God's word like so many, but in Christ we speak as persons of sincerity, as persons sent from God and standing in his presence.

Ash Wednesday is traditionally the time when we reflect on a solemn question. God has created us in love, and has given us his love in Christ; but, if we are honest with ourselves, there is a great deal in our lives that we might wish were otherwise. Fortunately, there are passages in scripture which reflect the same self-perception.

In the life of Paul, the moment *par excellence* when he faces his own fears and failures is 2 Corinthians. I am completely overwhelmed, he says, by all kinds of things—fightings without and fears within. He faces tensions in his own personal life, a sense of attack from people whom he thought were loyal to him, threats from people outside the church who are persecuting him.

The letter opens with an extraordinary picture of both the sufferings of Christ and the consolation of Christ. Paul has clearly experienced both of these in himself; so he begins (1:3–7) with a great prayer of blessing to God who is 'the Father of mercies and the God of all consolation, who consoles us in all our affliction, so that we may be able to console those who are in any affliction with the consolation with which we ourselves are consoled by God.'

This is the beginning of the great theme which will occupy us throughout Lent: 'As the sufferings of Christ are abundant for us, so also our consolation is abundant through Christ' (2 Corinthians

1:5). If we are being afflicted, it is so that we may be the instruments of consolation to others who are being afflicted. We see already a threefold movement in what is happening. First, the glory of Christ is revealed in Christ's own afflictions. Then, the knowledge of his suffering and resurrection comes to those who are called to be ministers of Christ: they will in turn suffer affliction, and know the consolation of Christ through that. Thus, as a consequence of who they are, and not just what they say, this sequence of affliction and consolation will be revealed to the world.

And so Paul writes in the first two chapters of 2 Corinthians about his own life. It is a life of pain and struggle, uncertainty and doubt, almost despair. Indeed, the only thing that keeps him from complete despair is his discovery that Christ is still in and with him then, and will bring him through suffering to consolation.

Today's passage (2 Corinthians 2:14–17) cannot be read as a casual statement of how God in Christ always leads us in triumph, as though Paul were strolling around the Mediterranean world as a kind of glorious hero-figure. We can only understand the triumphal procession if we read it in the light of all that has gone before, in the first two chapters of this letter. What he says is, like so much of 2 Corinthians, deeply ironic: as God is leading us in Christ through pain, through the valley of the shadow of death, through apparent despair, then somehow, strangely, as we look around, we discover that God is spreading in every place the fragrance that comes from knowing him (vv. 14–15), and we become the people through whom the sweet smell of God is actually being wafted to and fro. This seems to be a picture drawn from the use of incense in worship. As the beautiful smell permeates the temple, so the aroma of Christ is to permeate the world—through the life and suffering of the apostles.

Paul's point is that when people are in the presence of Christians, they should sense the presence of God. And it is part of the deal that, for at least half the time, Christians themselves are unaware that this is happening. As Paul found, he was simply aware of being unbearably crushed and seemingly destroyed. Nevertheless, as he looks back, he sees that this experience itself had to do with the aroma of Christ to God, the fragrant offering of Christ. It was part of the way in which the sacrifice of Christ was now embodied in the apostles.

There is an irony even within this, as he says in verse 16. When some people see the apostles going about in this way, all they can do is mock and say, 'Who needs a god like that? We want a real triumph. We want to be heroes. We don't want any suffering; we don't want any pain, so we're not interested, thank you very much.' This means, he says, that to some we are spreading a different sort of smell—the fragrance of death. They see the apostolic suffering and they turn away and say, 'No, that's not for us. What we want is a success story, from start to finish.'

But there are others who see it differently. They recognize that here is a depth, a power, a reality. Of such people, Paul says that to them we are 'a fragrance from life to life'; in our apparent suffering, dying and strange revival, we reveal to people the life and love of God. And as we today contemplate making these words our own, we are almost bound to say, with Paul in verse 16, 'Who is sufficient for these things?'

Paul is deeply aware that his vocation is to be the living embodiment of the outpoured love of God in Christ. He knows himself to be a sinner in general, and, worse, to have been a persecutor of the church; and then to have become a frail, fragile, often fearful apostle going about preaching the gospel, facing opposition, struggle and uncertainty, and not knowing what to do about it. He says, in effect: Yes, I am called to be an agent of Christ, part of the very body of Christ; and I recognize that I am unfit for a ministry like this. So, as he will say again and again throughout the passage, the sufficiency he has does not come from himself. It is the gift of God.

How are we to understand this? We cannot have a theology in which human beings, whether apostles or ordinary Christians, simply decide that they are going to pin their flag on God's map, and that they will attempt to do something, in their own strength, for God. What we have is a theology of vocation and enabling—a theology, in other words, of the Holy Spirit.

So, as Paul says in verse 17, we are not just 'peddlers of God's word'. We are not, like so many, going around hawking the gospel to anyone who cares to listen. Rather, we are speaking sincerely (v. 17), as persons sent from God and standing in his presence. Actually, the Greek is even tighter than that. Literally, it says '…as from God before God in Christ we speak'. That provides a very sharp definition of what it means to be an apostle, and what it means to be any Christian called to be Christ for the world: 'from God, in the presence of God, in Christ we speak'.

It is impossible to understand how this works without understanding the gift of the Spirit. That is, in part, what the next chapters of the letter are about.

Loving Father, release through us the fragrance of Christ to the world. Amen.

WEEK 1 (THURSDAY)

2 CORINTHIANS 3:1–6

Are we beginning to commend ourselves again? Surely we do not need, as some do, letters of recommendation to you or from you, do we? You yourselves are our letter, written on our hearts, to be known and read by all; and you show that you are a letter of Christ, prepared by us, written not with ink but with the Spirit of the living God, not on tablets of stone but on tablets of human hearts.

Such is the confidence that we have through Christ towards God. Not that we are competent of ourselves to claim anything as coming from us; our competence is from God, who has made us competent to be ministers of a new covenant, not of letter but of spirit; for the letter kills, but the Spirit gives life.

Paul is aware throughout 2 Corinthians that he is walking a very delicate tightrope. On the one hand the Corinthians are wanting him to be the sort of super-apostle about whom they can boast to their friends: 'You ought to see the man who runs our church. He's a great leader, a great speaker, a great hero-figure.' Paul cannot give them that kind of line because it would be a total falsification of the gospel—the gospel that focuses on the cross of Jesus. On the other hand, they have challenged him to explain himself. Why hasn't he visited them when he said he would? Why hasn't he done some of the things they thought he'd promised? And so he does want to explain certain things to them. But he has to do so without sounding as though he is merely recommending himself to them in the same way that some other teachers may have been doing.

Thus he begins chapter 3 by saying, 'Are we beginning to commend ourselves again? Surely we do not need, as some do, letters of recommendation to you or from you?' In the ancient world, as in some parts of the modern world, if you arrived in a community as a stranger, you expected to bring with you a letter from someone who would commend you. You may even have had a copy of your curriculum vitae, telling people what sort of a person you were. But Paul says, I don't need letters like that, because (here he is addressing the community: we can see him turning round and looking at them eyeball to eyeball) you yourselves are my letter of recommendation. This letter is written on my heart (and perhaps on 'your' hearts as well; there is a variation in the manuscript tradition at this point that may reflect a variation in Paul's mind). In other words, the Corinthians, and the memory of them, are engraved on Paul's heart. He preached to them, he watched them come to faith, he nurtured them, he loves them.

At the same time, he goes on to say that Christ, by the Spirit, has written the gospel on their hearts. They are, in both senses, known and read by all: all who see them can deduce that they are who they are because of Paul and because of Christ. This, then, is all the 'letter of recommendation' Paul needs: it is 'a letter of Christ, ...written not with ink but with the Spirit of the living God, not on tablets of stone but on tablets of human hearts.' (v. 2)

Paul has here grasped, and reused, a wonderful bit of Old Testament theology, namely one of the great promises in the book of Ezekiel. God, declared Ezekiel, would take out of your body the heart of stone and give you a heart of flesh (Ezekiel 36:26). Paul, characteristically, takes what he most wants to say to the Corinthians, and opens it up to reveal the depth of God's truth inside. In the Old Testament, God promised his people that the time would come when he would transform them so that instead of being his people in name only, they would be his people with a fresh dimension of reality above and beyond their human personalities. They would be the people on whose hearts God had written his law.

And Paul says: that has already happened to you Corinthians. You are not simply people who have heard a nice new idea, who have got a philosophy in your heads that you are now trying to think through, or perhaps to implement in your own strength. He says to another church on another occasion (1 Thessalonians 2:13), 'When you received the word of God that you heard from us, you accepted it not as a human word but as what it really is, God's word, which is also at work in you believers.' In other words, when Paul preaches the message, the Spirit of the living God is at work. The audience not only hears about Jesus Christ, in the sense of learning some truths about him. The personal presence and activity of Jesus Christ come to live within them. They become a letter of Christ to the world. They begin to embody Christ to the world.

So Paul takes a deep breath, and says (v. 4): that is the sort of confidence we have, through Christ, towards God. What has happened in Corinth is the result of Paul's apostleship. He doesn't have to drum up any other reasons for claiming apostolic authority there. The fact that a church exists in Corinth shows that Paul really is a minister of the new covenant, and he says again in verse 5, just as he said at the end of the previous chapter, 'Not that we are competent [or sufficient] of ourselves to claim anything as coming from us'; he insists to the Corinthians that he, Paul, as a human being, even as a Jew, as a Pharisee, with all his gifts and all his strength, is as nothing. All his competence, his sufficiency, comes from God. It is God who has 'made us competent to be ministers of a new covenant'—the new covenant that has been made by God in Christ, and is now sealed in the Spirit. This new covenant is a covenant not of the letter but of the Spirit.

This (in v. 6) is one of Paul's great 'Not... but...' sentences, which picks up not only Ezekiel but the whole train of thought in the Old Testament. Paul saw that God had given to Israel a blueprint for what it meant to be his people. And Israel chafed under this blueprint. Indeed, when Moses came down the mountain with the law, the first word of the law that Moses had to speak was a word of judgment, because the people had made the golden calf. From that moment there was an uneasy tension between the law as the *prescribed* way of life for the people of God and the *actual* way of life of the people of God. They were refusing to obey the law, going their own way, worshipping other gods and serving idols. Paul, as a Jew, was aware that the people of God as a whole were not what God wanted them to be. They needed that new covenant, that renewal by the Spirit, to enable them to be the light of the world, the bearers of glory, the people of God for the world.

And so Paul now says that God has made his commissioned apostles competent to be ministers of this new covenant in the

Spirit. The letter kills, but the Spirit gives life. The letter of the law says: this is the way of life for God's people, but without the Spirit you won't be able to keep to that way of life. So the commandment that promises life (which is why it was given) proves to be death for you. It merely shows up your failings. But instead, the Spirit now gives life. This is a typically dense little Pauline statement, and he is going to spend much of the rest of the chapter, indeed the rest of 2 Corinthians 3–5, unpacking and exploring it. The letter kills, but the Spirit gives life.

We have here a further unfolding of the theme which we saw earlier in 2 Corinthians. In Paul's own life, there was a sequence from despair to new hope, from death to new life. Paul saw that he had to endure this as a Christian, and as an apostle, and that the church had to endure it as the people of God in Christ. He sees, too, that the whole people of God, old covenant Israel to new covenant Israel, has to endure this same sequence, a sequence that is brought to its focus and climax in Jesus. It is the sequence of death and resurrection, of law and grace, of dying and rising in Christ, of Paul himself as an apostle suffering, even in the writing of this letter, and of the Corinthians being grasped by the strange message of death and new life.

As we begin to move on through Lent, we embrace the message of the cross because we know that at the heart of the message of Christ is also the new life of the Spirit. That is the message which will carry us forward through Lent, through this letter, and on towards Easter.

Enable us, Father, to serve you not in the letter but in the Spirit. Amen.

WEEK 1 (FRIDAY)

2 CORINTHIANS 3:7–11

Now if the ministry of death, chiselled in letters on stone tablets, came in glory so that the people of Israel could not gaze at Moses' face because of the glory of his face, a glory now set aside, how much more will the ministry of the Spirit come in glory? For if there was glory in the ministry of condemnation, much more does the ministry of justification abound in glory! Indeed, what once had glory has lost its glory because of the greater glory; for if what was set aside came through glory, much more has the permanent come in glory!

Paul's aim throughout the whole passage that we are studying is to explain to his puzzled and often muddled hearers the strange sort of glory that shines through his apostolic ministry. It isn't the sort of glory they had in mind, the sort of glory you associate with someone who strides around performing miracles, always a success, always living up to and beyond everyone's expectations. It is, rather, 'the glory of God in the face of Christ', as Paul will say later on.

To persuade them to see his apostolic ministry in this light, he begins with the contrast between the letter of the law and the gift of the Spirit. The 'letter of the law' is what was given through Moses on Mount Sinai, and for the rest of this chapter Paul has the picture of Moses in mind. During the wilderness wanderings, Moses used to go and speak with the Lord in the tabernacle; then he would come out and speak with the people. When Moses spoke with the Lord, his face shone. This made the people afraid, so he had to put a veil over his face.

Paul uses this somewhat puzzling picture of Moses as a way of showing that the revelation of God through the law was really a revelation of glory. We don't know what the Corinthians thought about the law of Moses; but Paul is emphasizing that, when God gave the law, it was a revelation of God's glory, and now, when the

Spirit is given, this must be a revelation of even greater glory. Despite appearances, in other words, what you see when the suffering apostle comes into town, with the marks of beating and stoning on him, is in fact the glory of God. The proof of this is that, when he preaches the gospel, God's Spirit is at work.

So, in verse 7, Paul says: when God gave the law it was an administration of death, because the people were not up to it. They couldn't obey the law, so it brought death to them. But it was, even so, an administration of glory so splendid that the people of Israel couldn't look at Moses' face because it shone so brightly. And he continues (v. 8): how much more then will the ministry of the Spirit come in glory?

He then, characteristically, explains this in more detail (vv. 9–11). If there was glory even in the ministry of condemnation, 'much more does the ministry of justification abound in glory!' Paul's ministry has been a ministry of bringing people, through the work of the Spirit, into the place where they are justified before God. That must be a revelation of glory, even though, with the suffering that goes with the preaching of the gospel, it doesn't look like it. 'Indeed,' he says in verse 10, 'what once had glory has lost its glory because of the greater glory.' The law is to the gospel like a flickering candle is to the sunrise. And what's more (v. 11), the law has now in that sense been set aside. The candle can be blown out, now that the sun has risen. Not that the candle was a bad thing, as we shall see. Paul never says that there was anything wrong with the law itself. It's just that, now, that which is permanent, namely the administration of the gospel, has come in glory.

What Paul wants his hearers to grasp is that they already have, in the gospel of Jesus Christ, all the glory they could possibly want. He will shortly explain that in more detail. But we can imagine the Corinthians being very puzzled, just as people today might be very puzzled. Outsiders often look at the church, full of muddle and sin and shame and half-heartedness and back-biting, and clergy who don't know what they're talking about and laity who go wandering off the point, and they say, 'Well, if that's all you've got to show for the wonderful message you talk about, you really are a muddled lot. How can you possibly be the body of Christ, the temple of the living God, as you say you are called to be?'

The answer comes again and again in 2 Corinthians. The glory of Christ is not revealed in spectacular show of success, in people who get everything right all the time. People like that, as we know, can sometimes be a pain in the neck. The church reveals the glory of Christ through suffering and shame as much as through what the world counts as success.

The way this happens is, often enough, that the church is called to be where the world is in pain, at the place where the world is suffering and in a state of shame and sorrow. The church is there as the presence of the suffering Christ in the world (a theme we shall pick up in a week or two's time). But for the moment we can rejoice in this, that the glory which is the gift of the Spirit is, quite simply, the gift of God's own life, the gift of justification over against condemnation. It is a revelation of God even more glorious than the glory of the law. And the law was so glorious that Moses' face was shining. Sometimes Christians' faces are shining. We may not be able to see it, but if we really believed we would discover that it is true.

Give us grace, Father, to see your glory in all those who believe and live the gospel. Amen.

Week 1 (Saturday)

2 Corinthians 3:12–17

Since, then, we have such a hope, we act with great boldness, not like Moses, who put a veil over his face to keep the people of Israel from gazing at the end of the glory that was being set aside. But their minds were hardened. Indeed, to this very day, when they hear the reading of the old covenant, that same veil is still there, since only in Christ is it set aside. Indeed, to this very day whenever Moses is read, a veil lies over their minds; but when one turns to the Lord, the veil is removed. Now the Lord is the Spirit, and where the Spirit of the Lord is, there is freedom.

Paul now picks up the picture of Moses veiling his face to shield the Israelites from the direct reflection of God's glory, in order to contrast his own ministry with that of Moses. The real contrast, however, is not between the law and the Spirit, nor simply between Moses and Paul. The real contrast is between the Israelites and the Corinthians. The Israelites were incapable of looking openly at the glory of God, but had to have it veiled. Paul insists, however, that the Corinthians are capable of looking directly at the glory of God. It is for this reason, he says, that he employs great boldness in addressing them face to face. 'Since, then, we have such a hope, we act with great boldness'. (v. 12)

'Boldness' is one of the big words in the early church. In the Acts of the Apostles the disciples are often said to speak with 'boldness'. The Greek word means 'open-faced' or, as we might even say, 'barefaced'. Someone who speaks with this 'boldness' can tell it like it is. Paul doesn't have to dress up the message with flowery rhetoric. He doesn't have to clothe the gospel in smooth speech to flatter a sophisticated audience, making them feel proud to be so clever. On the contrary, he can tell the story of the death and resurrection of Jesus, and the life of the Spirit, absolutely straight. This is why he draws a contrast with Moses (v. 13), who had to protect the people of Israel from the reflected glory, the glory that was ultimately set aside because of the fuller revelation of the glory of God in the gospel. Paul doesn't have to do this.

The reason for Moses' behaviour (v. 14) was that the minds of his hearers were hardened. We find in the gospels, in Paul, and throughout the New Testament, similar sorrowful statements about the condition of Israel. Paul knew that this had been his own condition before his conversion: he was apparently incapable of hearing the message of the gospel. So now he sees the Jews of Moses' day as incapable of responding from the heart to the message of the law. 'Indeed,' he says, 'to this very day, when they hear the reading of the old covenant [i.e. the Mosaic law], that same veil is there, since only in Christ is it set aside.' Paul believes that it is only in Christ and by the Spirit that people can come to a true understanding of the Hebrew scriptures themselves.

So, he says (v. 15), 'to this very day [Paul is thinking of life in the synagogue, which he knew well], whenever Moses is read, a veil lies over their minds.' Paul, with Christian hindsight, can see the whole story of the Old Testament pointing to the fulfilment of all God's promises in the Messiah. As he says earlier on in the same letter (1:20), in Christ all God's promises have their 'yes'. The synagogue community, however, are so unwilling to hear the message of the death and resurrection of Jesus that when they read the story, which reaches its climax with that message, they can't understand its true significance. But then, he says (v. 16), '...when one turns to the Lord the veil is removed.' He is here picking up the passage from the book of Exodus which says that when Moses went back to the tent to speak to God again he took the veil off so that he could speak with God face to face (Exodus 34:34).

And now comes the climax of this passage. 'The Lord is the Spirit, and where the Spirit of the Lord is, there is freedom.' In other words, Paul is saying: you Corinthians, and I as your apostle, can look one another in the face. We do not have to hide the glory. We are all reflecting it. (We shall explore this further tomorrow.)

Paul's appeal to the Corinthians is this: because the living God has been at work in you, through my ministry, by the Spirit, you and I have no need to hide from one another. We have no need to pretend. We have no need to dress up our message in fancy language to protect ourselves from the intimacy of the gospel, from the implications for us on a day-to-day basis. We can be honest and open with one another, because the Lord whom we all worship is the Spirit; and where the Spirit of the Lord is, there is freedom.

For Paul's Jewish contemporaries, the word 'freedom' meant, above all else, Exodus—being set free from Egypt and sent home to the promised land. Paul believes that the real Exodus has already happened in Christ. He says therefore to the Corinthians: don't be mistaken. You are already the free people, and I as your apostle share that glorious freedom with you. And this is what comes from being the people in whose hearts God has written his law by the Spirit.

This is the freedom on offer for all who are in Christ, who are indwelt by the Spirit.

Give to us and all your people, Father, the true freedom which is your will for all your children. Amen.

Week 2 (Sunday)

2 Corinthians 3:18

And all of us, with unveiled faces, seeing the glory of the Lord as though reflected in a mirror, are being transformed into the same image from one degree of glory to another; for this comes from the Lord, the Spirit.

In this remarkable verse, Paul draws the long argument of the chapter into a single condensed statement. The basic point he wants to make is simple, though startling. It is that when Christians, in whose hearts God has written his law by his Holy Spirit, are in one another's presence, they are beholding the glory of the Lord as they look at one another. This is the point of his image of the mirror: 'All of us, with unveiled faces, see the glory of the Lord as though reflected in a mirror.'

When Paul is looking at the Corinthians, he is, as it were, looking in an angled mirror: he looks at them and sees the glory of the Lord above and beyond them. The Spirit has worked in their hearts; whether they know it or not, they are reflecting the glory of the Lord. So too, says Paul, when you look at me as your apostle, as your suffering, beaten-up, ill-used apostle, you must learn to see the glory of the Lord in me. If, then, we all of us see this glory with unveiled faces, we act with great boldness. We do not have to hide things or cover things up. We are not like the children of Israel in the wilderness, who had to have the veil put over Moses' face because they couldn't bear to see the glory of the Lord. We are supposed to be able to take it. We are supposed to be able to recognize in this humiliation, in this suffering, that this is what the glory of the Lord actually looks like.

One of the basic laws of spirituality is that you become like what you worship. Thus, when people are gazing upon the glory of the Lord, they become transformed into the same likeness, transformed from one degree of glory to another. We often use this phrase 'changed from glory into glory' (as it comes in a well-loved hymn) quite casually, as though to mean that we will one day simply shine more and more like an electric light bulb. Now I do not doubt that what we shall be is yet to be revealed to us. There will be a radiance in the life to come which will revolutionize our understanding of light itself. But what Paul seems to mean here is that we are to be changed more and more into the image of Christ; and the image of Christ is precisely the image of the crucified and risen one. Thus, when we are together as Christians, and when the Spirit is at work in our hearts collectively, then by sharing in fellowship with one another we are not only encouraged by one another's faith but we are also being transformed so that we increasingly share the likeness of Christ. It is a transformation which, as he emphasizes at the end of the verse, comes from the Lord who is the Spirit.

This picks up what Paul has said in the previous two verses: 'When one turns to the Lord, the veil is removed. Now the Lord is the Spirit'. What he means is this: if we are to apply Exodus 34:34, on which verse 16 is based, we have to see it in terms of the Spirit. He is saying, in effect: if you want to know what it means to be a Christian, and if you want to know what it means to be part of the apostolic church, you must turn to the Spirit and find freedom there. Today we often use Spirit-language as a way of talking about spontaneity in worship or in prayer, as though that was all Paul had in mind. But he means something much deeper than mere spontaneity. He means liberation from the ministry of death; liberation from the need to pretend; liberation, in fact, to reflect the crucified and risen Christ to one another.

That, then, is the great emphasis of the whole chapter (2 Corinthians 3). Because God has written the law on the hearts of all his people by the Spirit, we are now the new covenant people. We are now transformed into the likeness of Christ. We must be sustained in this transformation by fellowship one with another. As far as Paul is concerned, this means that he recognizes the glory of God at work in the Corinthians and wants to encourage them to recognize that same glory at work in his own ministry.

Give us humility, Father, to see your glory reflected in others, and joy when others see it in us. Amen.

26

Week 2 (Monday)

2 Corinthians 4:1–4

Therefore, since it is by God's mercy that we are engaged in this ministry, we do not lose heart. We have renounced the shameful things that one hides; we refuse to practise cunning or to falsify God's word; but by the open statement of the truth we commend ourselves to the conscience of everyone in the sight of God. And even if our gospel is veiled, it is veiled to those who are perishing. In their case the god of this world has blinded the minds of the unbelievers, to keep them from seeing the light of the gospel of the glory of Christ, who is the image of God.

Paul had every reason to lose heart. There he was at Ephesus, all the news was bad, God seemed to have abandoned him, most of his friends were forsaking him, the churches where he had worked hardest had turned round and blown a raspberry at him, and he was ready to quit. Perhaps he thought bitterly of retiring back to Tarsus and writing a few books in his old age, complaining about how tough life was. God could finish the job.

But, despite everything, Paul doesn't do that. I suspect that many of us, faced with Paul's problems, would have done so. But precisely because his ministry is given to him by the mercy of God (v. 1), he does not lose heart. His ministry is grounded on nothing other than mercy, and so will ultimately contain nothing but mercy. And as he has received mercy, he forges ahead. We are not crushed, he says, we are not overwhelmed by the evil of the present situation. (That's what the word for 'lose heart' really means in the Greek.) He has this ministry, this service, as a special commission from God. It wasn't his idea, he didn't dream it up, but found himself commissioned in this way; he is not, therefore, at liberty simply to abandon it. God in his mercy has given it to him; he in his faithfulness is simply going to carry on.

As Paul does so, he learns that there is absolutely no point in trying to pretend that the gospel is other than it is. The gospel is all about dying and rising with Christ, and hence about the shame and humiliation that comes with being a Christian in the world, with being a minister of the gospel. He has renounced (v. 2) any idea of keeping the message secret. There were some philosophical teachers in the ancient Near East who tried to initiate people into secret cults, in which you would never tell your neighbours what went on because you were in truth rather ashamed of it.

What Paul does is out in the open. He can speak his gospel in the marketplace, in public. That is not to say that people will like it, or like him for saying it. But he has no need to be ashamed of it, as he says in Romans 1:16 ('I am not ashamed of the gospel of God'), and he refuses (v. 2) to practise cunning or to falsify God's word (one translation says 'to tamper with God's word'). There is always an insidious pressure on a Christian, perhaps particularly on an ordained minister, to fiddle the theological books, to go soft on the bits that our hearers might dislike. Perhaps we may be tempted to make the Bible, or the gospel, a bit more politically correct than it actually is. Paul says that there is just no point in doing that. What is needed, as in the second half of verse 2, is that 'by the open statement of the truth we commend ourselves to the conscience of everyone in the sight of God.'

This open statement of the truth is the real heart of evangelism. Evangelism is not persuading people that there is a new religious option that they might like to try out and see if it keeps them amused for a bit. It is the open statement of what God has done in Jesus Christ. Not everyone is going to like that. Many people find it deeply threatening to be told that the creator of the universe, the lover of the universe, is revealed in a crucified Jew in a backwater of the Roman Empire two thousand years ago. It was bad enough when it was only twenty-five years ago, as it was for Paul. This wasn't a message that made everyone jump up and down with excitement and say, 'Of course, how could we have missed it?' It was a message that would make the ordinary person in the street, Jew or Gentile, say, 'What rubbish! Why would the creator of the universe want to do such a thing?'

Paul sees this as evidence that the Christian gospel is also veiled. When you preach the gospel to outsiders, he says, it is like Moses declaring the law to the Israelites. If their hearts are hardened, all they will hear is a message which seems to have no bearing on their lives. That, Paul says in verse 4, is because 'the god of this world has blinded the minds of the unbelievers, to keep them from seeing the light of the gospel of the glory of Christ, who is the image of God.'

Paul of course knows perfectly well that, day by day in his own ministry, plenty of people in that category find the scales fall from their eyes as they did from his own. They suddenly come to see the truth, the glory of God in the face of Jesus Christ. But meanwhile, until that happens to them, this is the conclusion he draws: when people who have not heard the gospel before listen and respond with hostility or cynicism, what's actually happening is that they have so bought into the values of this world, the longing for success, fame and fortune, that the difference between their aspirations and the offer of the gospel is just too great. Straining their eyes for the former, they are completely blind to the latter. It is like someone who is tone deaf or colour blind listening to music or looking at a great painting. They just can't see what is attracting other people.

What is attracting people, as he says at the end of verse 4, is the light of the gospel of the glory of Christ, who is the image of God. This is an extraordinary statement to make about Jesus: that he is the image of God. On the one hand, of course, it means that Jesus Christ is the truly human being, as Paul puts it in various passages. As we shall see after Easter, Jesus Christ is the last Adam, the one who has inaugurated the new mode of human existence. At the same time, here and in Colossians 1:15–20, we find Christ as the image of God, the one who truly reflects God into the world. Just as by the Spirit we, warts and all, reflect God to one another, so Christ truly reflects the living God into the world. And the point of 2 Corinthians 4, as we shall see tomorrow, is partly to show that if, in Christ and by the Spirit, God has established the new covenant with his people, then now, in Christ and by the Spirit, this results in new creation. And just as Adam and Eve were at the heart of the first creation in Genesis 1, so Christ is the true human being at the heart of the new creation.

Give us patience, loving Lord, when people seem blind and deaf to your good news. Amen.

WEEK 2 (TUESDAY)

2 CORINTHIANS 4:5–6

For we do not proclaim ourselves; we proclaim Jesus Christ as Lord and ourselves as your slaves for Jesus' sake. For it is the God who said, 'Let light shine out of darkness', who has shone in our hearts to give the light of the knowledge of the glory of God in the face of Jesus Christ.

It seems that Paul is constantly being put on the spot by the Corinthians. They want him to speak about himself, to defend his own ministry, his own person, his own character. But he refuses to do this. At least, he refuses to do it in anything like the way that they would regard as valid. Instead, he offers himself, like John the Baptist offered himself, simply as a voice, a witness, a signpost.

Paul is who and what he is because he is a herald of the king, the Messiah. The word 'Christ', of course, means 'Messiah', which itself means 'King'. We should sometimes remind ourselves of that, perhaps by using a phrase like 'King Jesus' instead of translating it 'Jesus Christ'. Paul is a herald of the king: he travels around the ancient world, telling unsuspecting ex-pagans that there is another king, namely Jesus (Acts 17:7). So Paul himself is simply a slave, a servant (the word in Greek in verse 5 means 'slave'). We, he says to the Corinthians, are your slaves for Jesus' sake. We are simply here to serve you, to bring you the gospel, working as the go-betweens for yourselves and Jesus.

When that encounter has taken place, we can stand back and let you simply be yourselves, the people of God in Christ. What has been going on in Corinth through this whole process is nothing less than the outworking of God's new creation, and, as a result, the shining of God's glory. In verse 6 Paul quotes from Genesis chapter 1: God said 'Let there be light', and there was light. This same God who said 'Let light shine out of darkness', Paul declares, has now 'shone in our hearts to give the light of the knowledge of the glory of God, in the face of Jesus Christ'.

What is going on here? For Paul it is absolutely vital that what has happened in the gospel of Jesus is the beginning of God's new creation. The new creation began, as far as Paul was concerned, when Jesus of Nazareth came out of the tomb on Easter morning. The new creation will finally be fulfilled when the reign of Jesus in the present age is complete, and sin and death are fully overcome, so that, as he says in 1 Corinthians 15:28, 'God will be all in all'. The life of the church runs from that beginning of the new creation to the completion of the new creation.

This is enormously important for a number of reasons. To begin with, Christian spirituality is not an escape from creation. It is not a way out, a way of declaring the present world and our physical existence to be simply evil, dark, gloomy and bad, dragging our immortal souls down into the mire. On the contrary, God intends to redeem the present creation. He has begun that operation in Christ, and now continues it in the Spirit, in the hearts and lives and behaviour of those who are in Christ. And, as he does so, this means for Paul that God has shone into people's lives the light of the knowledge of the glory of God in the face of Jesus Christ.

Every element in this rich statement needs to be unpacked and laid out. Without Christ, people are in the dark. They don't know who they really are as human beings. They don't know who God really is. In particular, they cannot make any sense of the strange story of Jesus. But when God works through the preaching of the gospel, through the work of the Spirit, people come to understand all these things about themselves, about the world, about God and about Jesus. And supremely they come to the knowledge of the glory of God.

God's 'glory': the phrase means, no doubt, that when people eventually see God the sight is astonishingly bright and dazzling. But beyond that it also means that it is surpassingly lovely and beautiful. We don't talk as much about the beauty of God as we do about the glory of God, but glory surely embraces beauty, and a sense of awe and delight, as well as simply a sense of utterly dazzling light. And this is because God's glory, ultimately, is the revelation, the shining of who God actually is. In the gospel we discover that God is at heart the God of total self-giving love.

The experience is a bit like travelling alone, away from the people we love, and having nobody around with whom we can relax, with whom we can be friendly. And then somebody we know comes to meet us, in an airport or railway station, or when we finally arrive back home. Our hearts are warmed, deeply comforted, by this sudden presence of somebody with whom we can be truly ourselves, someone who will give themselves to us.

That is a very pale illustration of what it's like when you are away from God, not knowing who you are, not knowing who God is, and then you discover that the God who made the world is the God of utter self-giving love who longs to be there for you, to give himself to you and help you discover who you are. All of this is contained in the remarkable claim that 'God has shone in our hearts to give the light of the knowledge of the glory of God'. We can know God deeply inside ourselves, in the face of Jesus Christ, the crucified and risen one. When Paul says the word 'Jesus', he never forgets that this is the Jesus who died on the cross. If we want to know who God really is, we don't discover it by forgetting that Jesus died on the cross, by skipping past that and going on to what seems to us more obviously like 'glory'. We discover it as we look at the face which is crowned with the crown of thorns.

Standing back from this whole passage, we find that what Paul is trying to say to the Corinthians, and for that matter what we need to hear in the church today, is this: if we are to know God in Christ, and if we are to be the people that God wants us to be in Christ, we must learn the painful lesson of recognizing the glory of God, the god-ness of God, as we look at Jesus on the way to Calvary, and then finally on the cross itself. And part of this is learning that when, often to our dismay, we find ourselves called to follow in the way of the cross, that doesn't stop us from learning who God is. It doesn't mean that God has forsaken us. Times like these are the moments when we are privileged to be led by the Spirit, as Jesus himself was led by the Spirit, into the wilderness and along the way of the cross, a way illuminated by the knowledge of the glory of God.

When we are wandering alone and in the dark, gracious Lord, come to find us and greet us with your welcoming love. Amen.

WEEK 2 (WEDNESDAY)

2 CORINTHIANS 4:7–12

But we have this treasure in clay jars, so that it may be made clear that this extraordinary power belongs to God and does not come from us. We are afflicted in every way, but not crushed; perplexed, but not driven to despair; persecuted, but not forsaken; struck down, but not destroyed; always carrying in the body the death of Jesus, so that the life of Jesus may also be made visible in our bodies. For while we live, we are always being given up to death for Jesus' sake, so that the life of Jesus may be made visible in our mortal flesh. So death is at work in us, but life in you.

This is the point in the passage where Paul's actual situation, of which we must assume the Corinthians had some idea, comes to the fore. He is now talking straight to them about what he endured in Ephesus and elsewhere.

They have been ashamed of him. If he was a real apostle, he shouldn't have been suffering like this. He should have been able to pass through everything the world could throw at him, and escape unscathed. He should have been able to say a quick prayer, and find that God rescued him from all dangers and suffering. Instead, what has happened? He's been in jail; he's been beaten; and they've even heard that he's been depressed, upset and unhappy. And they can't understand what sort of an apostle could be like this. So Paul explains to them that the way he has come, the way that his apostleship has taken him, is no less than the revelation of the glory of God.

'We have this treasure,' he says, 'in clay jars'—the treasure of this gospel, this light shining out of darkness to give us the knowledge of the glory of God. We are battered old flowerpots filled with the glory of God, so that it is quite clear that the power and the glory belong to God, not to us. If Paul could snap his fingers, say a quick prayer, get out of jail free and go striding off regardless, how proud he would have become. How tempted he would have been to imagine that God was doing these things in him because he was special. And that of course is exactly what the Corinthians wanted—because they wanted it for themselves.

But Paul rules out this distortion of the gospel. We can be people who embody the gospel of Jesus Christ only if we are people who go through suffering, danger, difficulty and failure. When I read Terry Waite's autobiography some years ago, I was struck by the fact that, when he was finally released from his captivity in Beirut, he didn't come out with any huge new revelation, any vision of some new Christian philosophy. He simply came out as somebody who had said his prayers day by day, who had clung on by his fingernails to the love of God in Christ, and who was pretty much the man he was before his captivity, only now humbler and perhaps a bit wiser. I was horrified that many people, both inside and outside the church, seemed a bit ashamed of the fact that he had nothing more to say than that. To me it was a remarkable sign that he had gone to the place where the world was in pain, as an ambassador of the Christian church. He had taken some of that pain upon himself, and had managed to emerge at the end of it. It should have made the Christian church proud (in the best sense) to have among its numbers someone who would simply, humbly, go to the place of pain, and hold on to some of that pain *without knowing, particularly, what was going on.* 'We have this treasure in clay jars... We are afflicted in every way, but not crushed; perplexed, but not driven to despair; persecuted, but not forsaken; struck down, but not destroyed.'

Now the thing you have to realize about those verses (8 and 9) is that, while Paul was being afflicted, it felt as though he *was* being crushed. While he was perplexed, it felt as though he really *was* despairing. While he was being persecuted, it felt as though he *was* forsaken. While he was being struck down, he really thought he *was* going to be destroyed. It was a matter of surprise that he would turn round, a day or a week or a month later, and say, 'Extraordinarily, I still seem to be here. I haven't been totally crushed after all, though it felt like it at the time.' This is what it means (v. 10) to be carrying in the body the death, the dying, of Jesus, so that the life of Jesus may also be made visible in our bodies.

The suffering of the apostle is the means by which the gospel of Jesus is not just talked about but lived out at street level, at prison cell level. This is why, again and again, as the old saying goes, 'the blood of the martyrs is the seed of the Church'. It is when people are actually living out the dying of Jesus that, strangely but surely, the life of Jesus is also then made visible.

So he amplifies it in verse 11: 'While we live, we are always being given up to death for Jesus' sake, so that the life of Jesus may be made visible in our mortal flesh.' As he says in 1 Corinthians 15:22, 'As all die in Adam, so all will be made alive in Christ.' Again and again, it is when, in Christ, we share the death of Adam that somehow, strangely, we are brought through—and not just brought through ourselves, but enabled to be the glory bearers, the life bearers, the people at whom others look and discover what the gospel is all about.

As so often in Paul, we find a twist in the tail, this time in verse 12. 'Death is at work in us, but life in you.' What is he saying to the Corinthians? Is he perhaps teasing them, that they think that they must only have the *life* of Jesus, while all he has is the death of Jesus? He is, I think, challenging them, saying, 'Examine yourselves: have you, perhaps, too much triumphalist "life"? Have you never discovered what it means that you too should be bearing in your body the death of Jesus, so that the life of Jesus might be made visible in your mortal flesh?' This is, I suspect, at the heart of the message of Lent. This is, after all, the time when we can rediscover that only when we suffer with Christ will we learn what it means to be glorified with him.

Enable us, Father, both to recognize that we are clay jars and to celebrate the fact that you can fill us with your glory. Amen.

WEEK 2 (THURSDAY)

2 CORINTHIANS 4:13–15

But just as we have the same spirit of faith that is in accordance with scripture—'I believed, and so I spoke'—we also believe, and so we speak, because we know that the one who raised the Lord Jesus will raise us also with Jesus, and will bring us with you into his presence. Yes, everything is for your sake, so that grace, as it extends to more and more people, may increase thanksgiving, to the glory of God.

This passage is part of the radical application of Paul's great doctrine of 'justification by faith'. Paul is looking at his own constant suffering and trouble. He contemplates outward circumstances that would make anyone else despair. Because he is looking at all this through the eye of faith, however, he sees it differently.

What is 'faith'? For Paul, it is not a general religious attitude. It is faith in the God who raised Jesus Christ from the dead. Christian faith, certainly as Paul articulates it, looks through the lens of Jesus at who God is, and hence at what the world is, and hence at who we are ourselves. So he quotes from Psalm 116:10, 'I believed and so I spoke'.

In other words, when he speaks as an apostle, he is preaching the gospel on the basis of faith alone. He doesn't look at his own life and learning and say 'I'm such a clever fellow! I've got such a lot of wisdom! I'm just what the world needs!' Rather, he looks by faith at the God who raised Jesus; and, despite his own circumstances, huge problems, failures and fears, he continues to speak and announce the God who raised Jesus.

So, as he says (v. 13), 'We have the same spirit of faith that is in accordance with scripture—"I believed and so I spoke".' And Psalm 116 goes on: 'I kept my faith, even when I said, "I am greatly afflicted"; I said in my consternation, "Everyone is a liar."' Paul is thus evoking a passage which is itself about someone speaking from faith in the midst of troubles. Paul, as usual, is mindful of the context of what he is quoting, and so he continues, 'We also believe, and so we speak, because we know that the one who raised the Lord Jesus [i.e. God; this phrase, 'the one who raised Jesus', is a fairly regular Pauline way of referring to God] will raise us also with Jesus, and will bring us with you into his presence.'

This is clearly, again, part of Paul's view of what God has done and is doing by renewing the covenant in and through the Spirit. In Romans 8:9–11 Paul writes that the God who raised Jesus by the Spirit will also raise all those in whom the Spirit dwells. The Spirit is, in fact, the link between what happened to Jesus and what will happen to everyone who belongs to Jesus. That is why he can say (v. 14), '...the one who raised the Lord Jesus will raise us also with Jesus, and will bring us with you into his presence.' This relates closely to verse 12, where Paul said, 'death is at work in us, but life in you'. There is, I think, a deliberate irony here. Of course, he says, you Corinthians will be in the presence of God. You know that, and we are happy to affirm it. But in fact, even though death is at work in us, God will raise us and will bring us, with you, into his presence.

The focus of all of this—an emphasis which emerges particularly in Colossians, but which bubbles up in Paul all over the place—is that God's grace is designed to produce a *thankful* people. The rhythm of grace and thanksgiving—God's rich goodness, people's glad response—goes on and on, to the glory of God. Graciously, constantly, he works by the Spirit to create and call forth thankfulness from his newly created people. It is in this rhythm of grace that God is truly God, and, if we dare put it like this, that God *enjoys* being God.

In our day, just as people find it difficult to say 'sorry', so they find it difficult to say 'thank you'. And often, when people do say 'thank you', other people find it difficult to accept. We live in a society where we are all supposed to be self-sufficient, and everything done for others is a kind of a business deal. We have done our best to squeeze out the much richer, gentler, more powerful human interaction where someone acts out of sheer generosity and someone else accepts the action with open gratitude. We find it much easier to think of a network of obligations, rights and rewards than to imagine spontaneous generosity, seeking no recompense, and spontaneous gratitude, implying no inferiority or obligation.

What we have here, though, is the idea of a community where somebody, in this case God, does something out of sheer goodness, simply out of who he is. It is a community where people are so thankful that, without any diminution of who they are, but rather with an enlargement of who they are by their thankfulness, they respond to him in gratitude. This was, of course, a problem in the ancient world as well. So-called 'benefactors' gave gifts to people specifically in order to get a return, to enhance their social position, to look down their noses at those who benefited from their generosity.

But when God gives things, and indeed when God gives God's own self to people, it isn't like that at all. It is a glad outpouring of who God is, which should never produce guilty indebtedness. God wants us to be grateful, of course, but only because he wants to enjoy the relationship that is thereby created, together with the richer flowering of our genuine humanity.

At this point the argument of 2 Corinthians 4 turns a corner. Until now, Paul has been describing himself as deep in trouble, yet clinging to the belief that the life of Jesus will be made manifest in him, because he has borne in his body the death of Jesus. Now, however, he says 'Yes, and this is the faith that I have: that God, who raised Jesus, will also raise us with Jesus.' The whole drama is the story of grace, gratitude and glory. As so often in Paul, humans are caught up into this movement, into the great circle of grace. This is nothing other than the story of Christ, the Christ who came as the act and expression of God's grace, the Christ who embodied the perfect human gratitude and responsive self-offering to the Father, the Christ who now shares the Father's glory, indeed reflecting it perfectly because he is the truly human one. So none of the movement Paul describes is outside of Christ. It is all from the Father, through the Son and energized by the Holy Spirit. The more we read Paul, the more the doctrine of the Trinity appears to be necessary—not as an abstract philosophical deduction but as the deep inner meaning of life and the world.

Give us the gift, Father, of gratitude for all your gifts; that we may become more truly your children, and glorify you all our days. Amen.

WEEK 2 (FRIDAY)

2 CORINTHIANS 4:16–18

So we do not lose heart. Even though our outer nature is wasting away, our inner nature is being renewed day by day. For this slight momentary affliction is preparing us for an eternal weight of glory beyond all measure, because we look not at what can be seen but at what cannot be seen; for what can be seen is temporary, but what cannot be seen is eternal.

This passage is another transition point. Paul is now describing, more calmly, the whole state of affairs. He is not just talking about his own troublesome situation, but about the position of all Christians, looking at everything that the world can throw at them and yet claiming that God carries them through that and out the other side. This theme, for Paul, calls up the idea of the outer person and the inner person.

We have difficulty grasping what Paul means at this point. Old translations refer to 'the outer man' and 'the inner man'. Some of the new ones, anxious to avoid gender-specific language, say 'the outer *nature*' and 'the inner *nature*'. That can be misleading. Paul was not simply buying into the sort of scheme we find in much Greek philosophy, and in much popular thought today, in which the physical is bad and the non-physical is good.

As we shall see at the beginning of 2 Corinthians 5, Paul has no such dualism in mind. He is still thinking in a very Jewish way. As far as he is concerned, the created world is God-given. It happens to be the case, however, that the part of the created world we see at the moment is heading for decay, both in terms of human beings (as soon as we are born, we are on the way to death) and also in terms of the cosmos as a whole (our world is running down, and will, in a certain number of million years, cool down completely and lose its energy). The world, in other words, is good and God-given, but is impermanent. Without a great act of new creation by

God, human beings and the world as a whole will finally cease to be.

But Paul's whole point here is this: the God who performed the new act of creation through Jesus has now applied it to his people by the Holy Spirit. When we put the picture together we can say that though our outer nature is wasting away, our inner person, our true inner self, is being renewed day by day. This is why we don't lose heart. Whatever they do to Paul, whether they stone him or throw him into jail or whatever, he knows that the outward person was always heading for the grave. This merely proves the point. But God is at work by the Spirit, secretly, to do something quite new for us.

And what is it that God is doing for us? He is preparing 'an eternal weight of glory'. Translating this sentence (v. 17) is very difficult: literally, it reads something like 'For the temporary insignificance of our suffering is accomplishing in us an eternal weight of glory from one extraordinary degree to another.' Knowing what Paul went through, not least as he describes it in 2 Corinthians itself, it is astonishing that he can refer to all that suffering as temporary and trivial. As far as he was concerned, it didn't feel trivial when he was in the middle of it. Nor did it seem temporary. It seemed utterly crushing, and to be going on and on and on. But, as he looks at it in faith, he can say in all honesty that it is temporary and trivial compared with what God is going to do.

And what is God going to do? Ultimately, God is going to make his people truly human. This is the promise in Christ and by the Spirit. People often say, 'Oh well, I'm only human', by way of giving an excuse for poor behaviour. The implication is that being human is a somewhat shabby thing, and that the point of being Christian is to stop being human and to become something else instead. This is totally unPauline. Paul looks forward to the redemption, enhancement and glorification of his and other people's humanness.

'The weight of glory' thus seems to refer to a superabundant expression of that humanness: God's people will be more truly themselves. We sometimes speak of somebody who has been very sick being 'just a shadow of their former self'. But what Paul seems to be saying here is that human beings are just a shadow of their *future* selves. God has prepared a larger selfhood which is the true fulfilment of all that they are at the moment, which will be the final, glorious enriching of it. Everything that humans, at their deepest and best moments, are reaching out for, struggling after, longing for, and dreaming of, will finally be fulfilled. Not necessarily, of course, in the ways we would currently imagine; rather, in the ways that God knows will be truly fulfilling for us. So the 'eternal weight of glory' of which Paul is speaking is the new life, patterned on the risen humanity of Jesus, expressing not only what we are at the moment truly as God's children, as his creation, but what we shall be when God has completed what he has begun in the Spirit. As Paul says in Philippians 1:6, what God has begun in Christians he will bring to completion at the day of Christ Jesus.

The Christian's calling, therefore, is to look clearly at what cannot be seen, rather than at that which can. I am sure Paul was aware of how paradoxical that sounds. If something is invisible, the one thing you can't do is look at it clearly! But he is writing about a way of seeing with the eye of faith which looks both to the past (the resurrection of Jesus), the present (what God is doing by the Spirit), and the future (what God has prepared for his people). Once again, we find resonating throughout this whole chapter, and this whole section of 2 Corinthians, the sense of God's glory, the glory given to Christ, the glory given through Christ by the Spirit to God's people. Now that we have put the whole chapter together, we see that this is a glory which is already present, albeit in a mysterious way: when Christians look at one another, they can glimpse the glory shining from the face of the suffering one, the one who is sharing the pain of the world. That is the sign of the glory that is to come, when God finally swallows up death for ever and creates us as his renewed human beings. And that is the point to which Paul now turns, at the start of chapter 5.

Give us faith, gracious Lord, to look beyond the things we can see to the things we cannot; that, gazing with gratitude upon your glory, we may be prepared to share in it for ever. Amen.

WEEK 2 (SATURDAY)

2 CORINTHIANS 5:1–5

For we know that if the earthly tent we live in is destroyed, we have a building from God, a house not made with hands, eternal in the heavens. For in this tent we groan, longing to be clothed with our heavenly dwelling—if indeed, when we have taken it off we will not be found naked. For while we are still in this tent, we groan under our burden, because we wish not to be unclothed but to be further clothed, so that what is mortal may be swallowed up by life. He who has prepared us for this very thing is God, who has given us the Spirit as a guarantee.

When Paul says 'For we know...', I always wonder whether his hearers actually did know, or whether this is Paul's gentle way of saying, 'This is what I wish you knew—if only you remembered what I taught you and if you'd worked it all out'! In any case, here again he is referring to the larger truth that encompasses all the particular circumstances of his work, his mission, his suffering, his tribulation, his expectation. And this is one of those points where he draws back the veil from that which is yet to come.

He uses here the image of the 'house' or the 'tent'. Literally, he says 'If the earthly house of this tent is destroyed, we have a building from God, a house not made with hands, which is eternal, in the heavens.' There is a great deal going on here which needs unpacking.

To begin with, the language of 'tent' or 'tabernacle' or 'house' is all drawn from the Jewish temple. Paul is portraying the present human frame as a tabernacle, a tent, a temple for God in the Spirit. We know, he says, that this present 'temple' will be destroyed; but there will be a new temple. He is, of course, echoing the whole prophetic theme of the destruction and the rebuilding of the temple in Jerusalem. The death and resurrection of the people of God is, for Paul, the reality towards which the whole temple theme points.

The idea of a building 'not made with hands' is interesting because, for the Jews, whether or not something was made by hand had a very different meaning from the one it has for us. When we say today that something is 'hand-made' we mean it has been made with unique human attention, and not just by a machine. It is probably of rather superior quality, because someone has taken time and trouble over it. But the Jews use this language to speak of idols compared with the true God. That which has been made by hands is a mere idol. The true God is 'not made with hands'.

Paul's point is that the body we shall possess, in the new life that God will eventually give us, is the fuller reality to which the present body points. We are not to idolize the present body, its abilities, its status, and its honour and shame. The real thing is yet to come. And what is the real thing? Paul describes it as a house not made with hands, 'eternal in the heavens'. This idea of a building 'in the heavens' is very misleading to us. We may have been taught from an early age to think that the goal of the Christian life, towards which everyone is striving, is 'to go to heaven when we die'. The assumption then is that this 'building' is sitting up there in heaven, and that we go to heaven to enjoy it. But this image does not work like that at all. Indeed, throughout the New Testament we don't hear so much about going to heaven when we die, as about the new heavens and new earth that God will make. In other words, God's space and human space will be brought together and, as it were, married.

In this particular instance, the idea of the building 'in the heavens' is that it is waiting there, ready to be revealed when the time is right. Paul's doctrine of the resurrection does not talk about abandoning bodily existence and going off to a disembodied life. He describes the present body dying, and God giving us a new body or, even better, a renewed body, as our ultimate dwelling. This is the point made in chapter 5:2–4: in this tent, that is, in the present physicality, we groan because we long to be clothed with our heavenly dwelling—if indeed when we have taken off the present body we will not be found naked.

There are some problems of translation here, but the point is this: Paul is examining the possibility that, as Shakespeare's Hamlet puts it, we will 'shuffle off this mortal coil', and be left, presumably, with a naked spirit, a disembodied soul. That's still the conception of death that many people, including many Christians, have, but Paul rejects it. He says, in effect: no, that's not the point at all. We are indeed groaning at the moment, but this is not (v. 4) because we wish to be unclothed, but because we wish to be further clothed. We long for that which is 'mortal' (i.e. heading for death) to be swallowed up by life.

In other words, the future body is something greater, more glorious, than the present body. We are not expecting to become disembodied wraiths. We are expecting something that will be more glorious (corresponding to the weight of glory in 4:17) and more fully physical, more thoroughly able to resonate with the creative love of God.

And so, in chapter 5:1–4, Paul is insisting that this is why we do not lose heart. Although the present body is decaying, God has already prepared the new body for us. How can we be sure of this? Paul answers the question at the end of verse 5. 'He who has prepared us for this very thing is God, who has given us the Spirit as the guarantee' (or the 'down payment'). The Greek word for 'guarantee' is *arrabon*, the word used in modern Greek for an engagement ring. It is the object which certifies to the beloved that the promise is sure and will be accomplished. The same word was used in ancient Greek as a business term, for the 'down payment' which guarantees that the full amount will be forthcoming. The Spirit who is already at work, preparing this weight of glory for us, is the guarantee that the final new body will be ours.

In the midst of our present groanings, good Lord, give us courage and faith to believe that you are preparing for us a renewed body, that we may share the new life of our Saviour, Jesus Christ. Amen.

WEEK 3 (SUNDAY)

2 CORINTHIANS 5:6–10

So we are always confident; even though we know that while we are at home in the body we are away from the Lord—for we walk by faith, not by sight. Yes, we do have confidence, and we would rather be away from the body and at home with the Lord. So whether we are at home or away, we make it our aim to please him. For all of us must appear before the judgment seat of Christ, so that each may receive recompense for what has been done in the body, whether good or evil.

Having sketched a large picture of the ultimate purposes of God for his people, Paul now focuses on the way his own apostolic ministry belongs within these future plans and purposes of God. The tone is set right from the beginning: 'So we are always confident' (5:6). The word for 'confident' in the Greek comes right at the start of the verse; it could also be translated 'we are cheerful'. We have got accustomed, I think, in the Christian world, to supposing that if somebody tells us to be cheerful they want us to put on a large but possibly false grin. 2 Corinthians makes it clear that Paul wasn't that sort of person. Nevertheless, there was a deep cheerfulness about him, growing out of a knowledge that went below the suffering and the pain, a knowledge of who God was, in Christ, and what God was doing by the Spirit.

The reason he gives for his confidence, his cheerfulness, is that he recognizes the partial nature of the present situation. 'While we are at home in the body, we are away from the Lord'; but this will change. One day we will be with the Lord. The key to it all is found in verse 7: 'We walk by faith, not by sight.' We quite often say, 'Yes, I've heard of that person but I don't know him by sight', or, 'I've spoken to her on the phone, but I don't know her by sight.' Our knowledge of God is similarly 'not by sight'. Our knowledge of Jesus is 'not by sight'. We do, of course, know so much of Jesus, both historically through the gospels, and in the present by his Spirit, that seeing him, marvellous though it would be, would simply confirm what we already know. Nevertheless, seeing is what we long for, and the promise of it gives us confidence, as Paul repeats in verse 8.

As a result, Paul would rather be away from the present body and at home with the Lord. He says much the same in Philippians 1:23: 'My desire is to depart and be with Christ, for that is far better.' Many Christians have supposed that dying does not mean going straight to be with the Lord, but (maybe after a brief sight of him) spending a long period being purged, purified and made fit and ready; only then, after we have been kept waiting, in a considerable amount of pain and anguish, will we at last come home to be with the Lord. Paul knows absolutely nothing of that—and I'm convinced that he was not just speaking as if he were in a special category. He is talking about what is normal for all Christians: that we have confidence, and in that confidence we would rather be away from the body and at home with the Lord.

Then again, as in Philippians 1, he balances his longing to be 'at home with the Lord' with his determination to make the present life count in his service. However much he longs for the fuller life that is to be his, he does not have the right to decide when to leave the present one. There were philosophers in the ancient world who would regularly say, in effect, 'If you don't like the way things are at present, the door stands open.' Suicide was a well-known option, often regarded as noble and almost natural. For Paul, that decision is God's alone. So, he says, there is a task to perform in the present: 'Whether we are at home or away, we make it our aim to please him.'

There is a further misunderstanding to deal with at this point. Many young people in the modern western world find it, or at least believe it to be, very difficult to please their parents. Whatever we do just doesn't quite reach the high standard expected. Many continue through their whole adult life, even after their parents have died, still trying somehow to please them or at least appease them. Such people find the idea of pleasing *God* almost laughable. It seems quite impossible that God, being all-knowing and all-wise, could actually be *pleased* with them. You'd have to be an absolutely superb person on all fronts (they think) to please God.

The chances are that God would look down on their best efforts and say, 'Well, it's only nine out of ten, I'm afraid; that's not good enough.'

Clearly Paul does not look at the matter like that at all. For Paul, God is pleased when he sees his image being reproduced in his human creatures by the Spirit. The slightest steps they take towards him, the slightest movements of faith and hope, and particularly of love, give God enormous delight. However difficult we may find this to believe, not least because of our own upbringing, it is a truth that Paul repeats quite often. Who we are in Christ, what we do in the Spirit, is pleasing to God; God delights in us, and, like a parent, he is thrilled when we, his children, take even the first small baby-steps towards the full Christian adulthood he has in store for us.

When we reach the solemn and serious verse 10 ('All of us must appear before the judgment seat of Christ, so that each may receive recompense for what has been done in the body, whether good or evil') we might incline to a certain Christian approach that is somewhat misleading.

If we have been well taught that we can never 'make ourselves right' before God, we might assume that there is nothing good about us, that when we finally stand before God we will have nothing to commend us to him. That is not, however, the way Paul sees it. For Paul, if we are genuinely living in and by the Spirit of Jesus, then day by day, often without our even realizing it, we will have done many things that will give God pleasure—the smallest act of forgiveness, a great act of justice or mercy, a wonderful act of creativity enriching God's world. As a result of all these many things God will say, 'Well done, good and faithful servant.' When he says that, of course, we will rightly say, 'Our competence, our sufficiency, comes from God.' We never escape the wonderful circle of grace, gratitude and glory. None the less, it really will be us whom God thanks, us whom he praises.

Although in these days of feeble relativism it is important to stress that God is indeed the judge who cares passionately about good and evil, and that he is a just God who will not allow sin for ever to flourish unchecked, we must remember that the warning of final judgment should not make Christians gloomy or anxious. We are not supposed to drag ourselves through our lives thinking,

'Have I made it? Will I be all right?' We have assurance in the gospel that because Jesus died for us and rose again, we are completely forgiven and accepted in him. This assurance is matched by the delight we can and should take in the work of the Spirit. Through the Spirit we are enabled to do many things by God's grace so that, when we appear before the judgment seat of Christ, we will find we have pleased him in countless ways that for now we can only guess at. Of course, this is by no means the last word on the final judgment, but unless the assurance forms part of the picture the whole story has not been told.

Take delight, dear Father, in us your children; give us courage to believe that you are pleased even with our small and timid steps to follow Jesus; and help us to know the joy of your approval. Amen.

WEEK 3 (MONDAY)

2 CORINTHIANS 5:11–15

Therefore, knowing the fear of the Lord, we try to persuade others; but we ourselves are well known to God, and I hope that we are also well known to your consciences. We are not commending ourselves to you again, but giving you an opportunity to boast about us, so that you may be able to answer those who boast in outward appearance and not in the heart. For if we are beside ourselves, it is for God; if we are in our right mind, it is for you. For the love of Christ urges us on, because we are convinced that one has died for all; therefore all have died. And he died for all, so that those who live might live no longer for themselves, but for him who died and was raised for them.

Paul comes back, in a large circle, to the question of what it means to be an apostle. He has been challenged on whether he is a true apostle, because he doesn't conform to the Corinthians' expectations; he has explained to them in chapter 3 that his apostleship is a ministry of the new covenant, and that therefore, whether it looks like it or not, it is a ministry of glory. He has explained to them in chapter 4 that this glory is not undermined by the fact that he suffers terrible pain and torture; rather, it is shown up more fully. The glory consists precisely in bearing in his body the death of Jesus.

He has now set that extraordinary picture against the glorious backcloth of God's ultimate restoration, God's putting all things to rights (the true meaning of 'judgment'). On that basis he says, 'Now you can understand why I do what I do as an apostle.' As he says in verse 11, 'Knowing the fear of the Lord, we try to persuade others.' Knowing who God is, our job, he says, is to persuade other people to see the world, and God, and Jesus, as we have learned to do. In the middle of this, however, he says, in effect, 'And God knows perfectly well who we are being and what we are doing in and through this whole process.' Paul's sense of identity is not determined by what the Corinthians think about him. It is determined by God's knowledge of him.

He is still reminding them that they may need him to commend himself but that God has no need of such things. 'I hope,' he says, 'that we are also well known to your consciences'; in other words, I hope you can see what is actually going on in my life and that what I am saying is the truth. He insists in verse 12, 'We are not commending ourselves to you again.' There is more than a touch of irony here: he both is and is not commending himself to them. 'We are giving you an opportunity to boast about us, so that you may be able to answer those who boast in outward appearance and not in the heart'; this should be read (as we would say) with tongue in cheek, though the underlying point is serious. Paul is hinting that some teachers in Corinth are saying that what really counts for apostleship is a good outward showing. It is possible that they are Jews who are insisting, like the false teachers in Galatia, on an 'outward showing in the flesh', that is, circumcision. Or they may be teachers who are encouraging the Corinthians to indulge in some spectacular form of spirituality, or socially advantageous 'wisdom' teaching.

Whoever they were, Paul wanted the Corinthians to have an answer about the nature of his own apostleship to give to such false teachers. The Corinthians may have been taken in by the false teachers, and Paul is offering them a challenge. He presents it in the form of the help they need for the debate in which they ought to be engaged. He wants them to be able to explain, to anyone who challenges them on the matter, why it is that their apostle, their founder, cuts such a poor figure when he shows up in town.

This leads him to the heart of the matter, in verses 13 and 14, where we discover the essence of all Christian ministry, in Paul's day or our own. 'If we are beside ourselves, it is for God; if we are in our right mind it is for you. For the love of Christ urges us on.' At the centre of Paul's life is the strong sense of being grasped by the love of God in Christ. He is so filled to overflowing with the sense of God's love, revealed in the death of Jesus and now poured out by the Spirit, that sometimes when he is speaking he is swept away, forgetting the normal rules of rhetoric. He isn't making the proper sort of speech that they would expect a good Hellenistic orator to make. And he admits it: all right, so I am beside myself;

but this is because of the love of Christ, and it is for the glory of God. And if I am speaking soberly, if I come down from that level, this is for your sake. This last is perhaps a slight put-down for the Corinthians. He is implying that when he is in full flight, forgetting social conventions and letting the love drive him on, this glorifies the living God, but he has to come down to their mundane level and be 'in his right mind' to clarify things for them.

His central point is love: '...the love of Christ urges us on'; the love of Christ controls or constrains us. This love is the motor that drives him, the passion that fuels him, the goal towards which he strives, the mark at which he is aiming. And what energizes this love? 'We are convinced that one has died for all; therefore all have died.' When Paul looks at the church in Corinth, he sees them collectively and individually as persons for whom Christ died, and therefore as people loved by the one who has also loved him. He seems to look wider, too, than just the church. When he comes into a new town, where nobody has heard the name of Jesus before, he sees people for whom Christ died. His longing is to explain to them how deeply they are loved, in Christ, by the living God.

The result is (v. 15), '...so that those who live might live no longer for themselves but for him who died and was raised for them.' Paul now pulls the whole argument together. The reason Christ died was in order to create a family who would take their part in this rhythm of grace and gratitude and glory. Those who are grasped by the love of Christ, whether they are apostles or existing church members or new converts, will see their lives as no longer their own but held in trust, to be lived in gratitude for God's grace and in the hope of God's glory. Once again, as so often, he brings the whole argument back to Christ. The aim is that all should live 'for him who died and was raised for them'.

Sweep us away, Lord Jesus, with your love, that we may overflow in love to all we meet. Amen.

Week 3 (Tuesday)

2 Corinthians 5:16–19

From now on, therefore, we regard no one from a human point of view; even though we once knew Christ from a human point of view, we know him no longer in that way. So if anyone is in Christ, there is a new creation: everything old has passed away; see, everything has become new! All this is from God, who reconciled us to himself through Christ, and has given us the ministry of reconciliation; that is, in Christ God was reconciling the world to himself, not counting their trespasses against them, and entrusting the message of reconciliation to us.

Paul continues to develop his explanation of why his apostleship is as it is. He now turns to the question of how he regards people, what criteria he uses to assess them. When he looks at people, he no longer sees them in terms of human status or prestige, in terms of what we would call their natural abilities, whether they can speak well or even live well and happily, let alone their financial circumstances, or social class. He now sees quite differently.

Once, he says in the second half of verse 16 (presumably referring to the time when he was still an unconverted Pharisee), he judged Jesus that way. He assessed him as a Galilean carpenter, without proper rabbinical training, leading a strange rabble with a bizarre agenda, finally put to death by the occupying forces. He thought he could tell, as a Jerusalem-educated Pharisee, that somebody like that was without value. The fact that the Romans executed him merely proved the point. Ah, Paul says, but that was to look at the Messiah from a thoroughly human point of view. We no longer look at him like that, because God raised Jesus from the dead; and that opened to Paul a whole new perspective on who Jesus was, who God was, and who Paul himself was, and what the world was.

And now, Paul looks at human beings, men, women and children, and sets aside the normal categories by which we judge one another. Rather, as he says in verse 17, 'If anyone is in Christ, there is a new creation.' Some translations use phrases such as 'If anyone becomes a Christian, they become a new person inside.' That is a true statement, but the Greek that Paul uses here says something larger, simpler and stronger: 'If anyone in Christ—new creation.' In other words, when someone believes the gospel and is baptized, another part of new creation bursts in upon the world. New creation happened when Jesus of Nazareth rose from the dead. By God's Spirit, it happens again every time somebody becomes a Christian, and will go on happening until the new creation is complete, and God is all in all.

As a result, '...everything old has passed away; see, everything has become new' (v. 17b). Some manuscripts miss out the 'everything' here, so the sentence reads, '...the old has passed away, and it has become new'. This points us to the end of the book of Revelation, to the one who says, 'Behold, I make all things new.' The new creation is a spectacularly important doctrine. So many Christians miss out on it, because they assume that our ultimate goal is to escape this present world and go to a better one, somewhere totally different. A lot of our hymns, our prayers, and sadly even some sermons, speak in that language, which is not the true New Testament vision.

The New Testament vision is of the present creation being recreated, being made new, by God. This newness is already anticipated, already breaking into the world when people are joined to Christ in baptism and faith, and live by faith in Christ. It breaks in when people, by the power of the Spirit, perform acts of new creation, by writing a symphony or a poem, by working to protect the environment, by struggling for justice and protection for the vulnerable, by building up communities, by holding at bay all the forces of destruction which threaten human lives and societies.

Paul's specific task is described as the work of reconciliation. The world is out of tune with God, its maker. How and why that is so is a deep and dark mystery. At the heart of Jewish and Christian theology is the story of how God made a world distinct from himself, and how this world, tragically, has gone its own way. Now it is not merely distinct from God; it is in rebellion against God, though still loved by him. What God has done in Christ is to turn the world gently round to face him again. In his great love, his desire is to smile the world back into new life. He gazes at his world with the love which shines from the cross, from the dying and rising Christ. And this gaze of God is communicated through the work of the apostles.

That is why, as Paul says, this whole ministry is 'all from God'. God has 'reconciled us to himself through Christ, and has given us the ministry of reconciliation.' There in verse 18 is the two-stage plan of God for reconciling the world. God, like a great physician, has prepared the medicine that he knows will heal the disease, and when the first people have been cured he summons them to be doctors, to go and apply this medicine to everyone else who needs it. And then, in the spectacular climactic statement in verse 19, he explains, 'In Christ, God was reconciling the world to himself, not counting their trespasses against them, and entrusting the message of reconciliation to us.'

The living God was present and active in Jesus the Messiah, Jesus the crucified and risen one. Here is one of the many, many statements Paul makes to show clearly that God loved the world too much to send somebody else. God so loved the world that he came himself, in the person of his Son, the Messiah, to reconcile us to himself. In this way evil would no longer count against the world and all of us who live in it. The apostles, and then an ever-increasing number of people, would be caught up in the work of bringing that message of reconciliation to the world. At the heart of Paul's self-understanding is this vocation and commission: to tell the world that the creator of the world is also the lover of the world, and that he has, in Christ, already achieved the work of reconciliation.

Holy Spirit, breath of the living God; renew me, and all the world. Amen.

WEEK 3 (WEDNESDAY)

2 CORINTHIANS 5:20–21

So we are ambassadors for Christ, since God is making his appeal through us; we entreat you on behalf of Christ, be reconciled to God. For our sake he made him to be sin who knew no sin, so that in him we might become the right- eousness of God.

In the last two verses of 2 Corinthians 5, Paul draws together the threads of his whole discussion in the previous three chapters. He describes himself as 'an ambassador for Christ'. For Paul, we must remind ourselves, the word 'Christ' was not simply a proper name. It was a royal title. 'Christ' was the Messiah, the king, the King of Israel; hence, as the psalms and the prophets always indicated, he was the King of the world. As far as Paul was concerned, Jesus the Messiah had been exalted as the ruler of the universe.

So when Paul engaged in his work, his apostolic ministry, he wasn't simply offering people a new religious option. He was acting as an ambassador for their rightful king. The ambassador in this case was not presenting a threatening message, as ambassadors sometimes did. Nor was he offering a cold and formal treaty. He was holding out the offer of peace, the chance of reconciliation, the right hand of friendship. The flavour of the passage is this: the king of the world has sent a message from his father, the creator God, and he is sending that message through his ambassadors. 'On behalf of the king we are ambassadors, as though God himself were making his appeal through us.' (v. 20)

In the second half of verse 20, therefore, Paul is not summing up his message for the benefit of the Corinthians, as they have already been reconciled to God. The word 'you', which appears in some translations at that point ('we beseech *you* on behalf of Christ'), doesn't actually occur in the Greek. Paul is not addressing the Corinthians; he is telling them what his message is to the whole world: we are beseeching people on behalf of the king, on behalf of the Messiah, that they, the people out there in the world, should be reconciled to God.

He then sums up, in verse 21, the reason why this is the case. In addition, he once again draws into a characteristically compressed and dense statement the way he sees his own ministry of the grace and love and message of the Gospel. 'For our sake (God) made him to be sin who knew no sin, so that in him we might become the righteousness of God.'

This phrase 'the righteousness of God' has caused a great deal of puzzlement, both in this passage and in its various occurrences in the letter to the Romans, where it is one of the major themes. People have wondered whether this 'righteousness of God' is a quality of God himself, or a status that God gives to people, or perhaps a system whereby God saves people. Some have even seen it as a moral quality of Christ, which is somehow transferred or 'reckoned' to individuals when they become Christians. It is clear from the letter to the Romans, however, that what Paul means by 'the righteousness of God' is God's faithfulness to his covenant. God made covenant promises to Abraham, Isaac, and Jacob; he repeated those promises in various ways through Moses and David; now God has, in Jesus Christ, finally and fully been faithful to that covenant. What God intended to do to and through Israel, to make Israel his people for the world, God has now achieved and accomplished in Jesus Christ. That is the message, particularly, of Romans 3:21 through to 4:25.

So when Paul employs the same phrase here, we can understand it in the light of that fuller exposition in the letter to the Romans. What then does he mean when he says '...that we might become the righteousness of God'?

He is not simply making a detached statement of how the atoning work of Christ on the cross affects individuals (which is how it has often been understood). It is of course true, as far as Paul is concerned, that on the cross Jesus Christ bore the full brunt of evil and its consequences, so that the world could be free. But the last three chapters of this letter have been about something else. What we should expect at this summarizing moment, and what we in fact get from Paul, is a further statement of how his apostolic ministry functions within the purposes of God.

In the first half of the verse ('For our sake he made him to be sin who knew no sin') he asserts that God has, in Christ, dealt with the sinfulness of humanity—including the sinfulness of the apostles. Paul looks back at his own past and knows that he had been an utter rebel against God and against the gospel, not least in having been a persecutor of the church. He knows, as he says in 1 Corinthians 15:9, that he is not worthy to be an apostle, but in order to fit him for this work, God has dealt with his past. And in the same way God has made Christ to be sin for us all, even though he himself was sinless.

The aim of this was, as in the second half of the verse, so that we might embody the covenant faithfulness of God in Christ. What does this mean? It means, as we have seen throughout the last three chapters of the letter, that Paul was coming to embody the covenant purposes of God, not only in his words, but in his life, his actions and his suffering. The point he is making here is quite sharp: when the Corinthians were faced with him, they were not simply meeting some unlikely person who happened to be preaching the love of God. They were meeting someone who, in his own body, in his very person, was demonstrating the fact that God was, in Christ, faithful to his covenant promises.

In other words, Paul's own suffering, and also the fact that he could endure this suffering (persecuted but not forsaken, perplexed but not driven to despair, and so forth), are the signs that he was embodying the covenant faithfulness, the covenant love, of the living God. This verse is not simply a detached statement of atonement theology. It is a summary of everything that Paul has been saying in the letter so far.

Thus, if the Corinthians understand who he is and the true nature of his calling, they will realize that Paul's suffering, and the problems of which they are tempted to be ashamed, are actually the mysterious revelation—just as Christ on the cross was a mysterious revelation—of the secret but powerful and loving purposes of God, who saved not only them but the whole world. Perhaps we can also hear in this the hint of a challenge. If Paul is calling the Corinthians to prepare themselves to become embodiments of the covenant faithfulness of God, there may be a similar challenge for us as well.

Open our ears, Father, to hear your commission to us, that we should be ambassadors for Jesus, our Lord and King. Amen.

WEEK 3 (THURSDAY)

2 CORINTHIANS 6:1–2

As we work together with him, we urge you also not to accept the grace of God in vain. For he says, 'At an acceptable time I have listened to you, and on a day of salvation I have helped you.' See, now is the acceptable time; see, now is the day of salvation!

Paul has now set out the whole theology of what it means to be an apostle. He has explained to the Corinthians the reason for what he is doing, and how it fits into the large-scale plan of God, the revelation of the love of God in Christ, the glory of God seen in the face of Jesus Christ and reflected in the apostolic ministry. He now turns to address the Corinthians specifically, and says, 'In all this, we are working together with God; and we urge you not to accept the grace of God in vain.'

He is worried that they will have been seduced into other ways of thinking, ways that come insidiously from their own culture. Although they have accepted the grace of God, they may find that it all comes to nothing, that they will be unable to carry forward the work of God in Christ, because they are, instead, working in a different direction, working to boost their own pride, to be acceptable to their peers in society. This may perhaps also reflect the ideas and philosophies of some of the teachers who had followed Paul around, and whom he discusses later in the same letter. So he here urges the Corinthians to grasp the grace of God.

For Paul, 'grace' is shorthand for 'what God has done in Jesus Christ', a word with which he draws together the whole sequence of thought about what the creator God has done for the world in Israel, in Christ and in the Spirit. Yes, he says, you have accepted this gift, this grace; but now you have to make it real, to work it out, to see what it means in practice. And he quotes from a wonderful passage in the Old Testament which, as we know from many parts of Paul's writings, was never far from his mind: Isaiah 40–55. These chapters describe the outpouring of God's covenant love through the work of the Servant of the Lord, who would accomplish God's purpose through his death and resurrection—in other words, the very matter that Paul has been expressing.

He quotes from Isaiah 49:8: 'At an acceptable time I have listened to you; on a day of salvation I have helped you.' Here, as throughout his writings, Paul is saying: 'Now is the time when the promises of scripture are being fulfilled.' His theology is comprehensible only if we realize that, for him, the life, teaching, death and resurrection of Jesus Christ meant that all the great promises of scripture came true. It was not just one or two, leaving Paul with the majority of them still waiting to be fulfilled. Far from it: he sees that in Christ, as he says in 1:20, every single one of the promises of God have found their Yes. He can therefore say to them, 'See, now is the acceptable time; see, now is the day of salvation.' This now is what the prophets were talking about; they must not be slack in grasping the promises of God or, rather, being grasped by them. They must in turn be people in whom the grace of God is at work, revealing his glory to the people in their society. Just as Paul had been the embodiment of God's love and grace and glory to the Corinthians, so now he is determined that they shall embody these wonders to their own communities.

They cannot do that by simply conforming to the pressures of society, by trimming the sails of their Christian message to the prevailing wind of their surrounding culture. They can only do it if they realize that the purposes of the God of Israel, the God who made those promises through prophets like Isaiah, have come true in Jesus Christ, and that the promises are true for them now and also through them for others. 'Now is the acceptable time, now is the day of salvation.'

Nowadays we sometimes find this quite difficult to grasp. We are inclined to say, 'So Paul said that two thousand years ago, and here are we still bumbling along. Have we really advanced very far?' I think we need to lift up our eyes and see what the gospel has actually done. We need to remind ourselves, as the psalmists were fond of doing, of what God has already accomplished. We need to recognize the many thousands of ways, and many millions of lives, in which God's grace in Christ has been revealed over the last two thousand years. His glory has been seen in the gospel, and he has been praised and worshipped by glad and renewed people of every race. We need to recollect that our vocation is to act as conduits for the grace of God. Having accepted the gospel revealed in Jesus Christ, we must recognize that today is the day for choosing this vocation. God wants us today to put into practice his grace not only in our lives, but also in the communities in which we live.

Pour out your grace, Father, not only to us but through us. Amen.

WEEK 3 (FRIDAY)

2 CORINTHIANS 6:3–10

We are putting no obstacle in anyone's way, so that no fault may be found with our ministry, but as servants of God we have commended ourselves in every way: through great endurance, in afflictions, hardships, calamities, beatings, imprisonments, riots, labours, sleepless nights, hunger; by purity, knowledge, patience, kindness, holiness of spirit, genuine love, truthful speech, and the power of God; with the weapons of righteousness for the right hand and for the left; in honour and dishonour, in ill repute and good repute. We are treated as impostors, and yet are true; as unknown, and yet are well known; as dying, and see—we are alive; as punished, and yet not killed; as sorrowful, yet always rejoicing; as poor, yet making many rich; as having nothing, and yet possessing everything.

Paul now returns yet again to the theme of his own ministry. He wants to make clear to the Corinthians the basis on which he is appealing to them, and to explain the nature of his appeal. He wants them to be his partners in a ministry that reflects and reveals the glory of God in the crucified and risen Jesus. He tries to remove every obstacle from the way of his vocation, and he wants them to do the same.

So he begins (v. 3), 'We are putting no obstacle in anyone's way, so that no fault may be found with our ministry.' The Corinthians had found plenty of fault with Paul's ministry, precisely because it didn't conform to the sort of social and rhetorical standards that they were expecting. Paul knew, however, that the true potential obstacle to his ministry was the danger that he might fall short of fully embodying the love of God as seen in the cross. He says (v. 4), 'As servants of God we have commended ourselves in every way.' Building once again on chapters 3 and 4, he shows that he has commended himself as a true apostle, not by showy, flashy rhetoric, or by conforming to the standards of speech-makers in their society, but by reflecting in his own life the pattern of Jesus Christ.

He explains this with a list of what he has done and endured. There is, perhaps, a deliberate irony in his use of quite fine rhetorical technique in this list. It begins in verse 4, and runs on to verse 10, with the first two verses speaking of afflictions, hardships, calamities, beatings, imprisonments, riots, labours, sleepless nights, and hunger.

We get a clear picture here of what it was like for Paul journeying around the Mediterranean world. If today we follow in his footsteps, as tourists or pilgrims, we stay in hotels and go on well-organized transport with guides to show us around. For Paul there was always danger. There were robbers on the road; people were liable to set upon him. If he was on a boat, there might be storms, and they didn't have the kinds of safety mechanisms that we take for granted today. Day by day, night after night, Paul knew what it meant to sleep and rise with no human means of support, no human securities. If he was carrying money with him, it might be stolen while he slept. He had to go hungry, to travel when he was already exhausted, press on without rest. At the same time, however (v. 6), he commends himself 'by purity, knowledge, patience, kindness, holiness of spirit, genuine love, truthful speech and the power of God'.

These verses give us an extraordinary contrast between the outward circumstances of the apostle and his inward serenity. The outward circumstances were enough to throw anyone into despair, but within we have a sense of Paul's vocation: at every moment he had to be pure, he had to be one who walked closely with God, who was patient, who was kind.

A note about kindness: we sometimes forget that kindness was not a highly prized virtue in the ancient world. You were considered smart and clever if you looked after Number One; if you have any energy left from that, you might, perhaps, be nice to those with whom you lived, your close friends or relatives. For Paul, though, kindness was a key Christian virtue, because it reflected the generous, self-giving love of God in Christ.

The catalogue continues. Paul also had to be holy in his whole approach to everybody whom he met. He had to offer genuine love, not forced (people see through that extremely quickly), but welling up because of the Holy Spirit who had been given to him. He had to tell the truth at all times; again, people soon learn whom they can trust always to do that. These are the simple, clear, tough, demanding and very revealing characteristics that mark out the genuine apostle. And, as he lived all of these things, he was aware of 'the power of God' at work within him, so that even if he was set upon by robbers, or in danger of shipwreck, he trusted God to be with him and protect him.

Paul then anticipates that fuller statement of 'the whole armour of God' which he expounds in Ephesians 6:11–17. Here he speaks of having (v. 7) 'the weapons of righteousness for the right hand and for the left'; once more, 'righteousness' is not simply a moral quality, a cold, formal 'goodness' (which is what the word so often means for us), but has the Jewish resonance of 'covenant faithfulness'. It refers both to God's covenant faithfulness to Paul and also to Paul's determination that, grasped by that faithfulness, he would himself remain loyal to God's covenant. He would be a loyal minister of the gospel to all those whom he met, on the right hand and on the left—or, as we might say, wherever he turned.

What did he have to put up with as a result of all this? Verses 8–10 give the answer: 'with honour and with dishonour'. Some people thought he was tremendous; others thought he was a complete waste of time. 'In ill repute and good repute': in some places he would hear people whispering in the streets, 'Who is this strange fellow? Some odd, wandering Jewish speaker, and we don't understand what he's talking about. He's probably up to no good.' In the next street he might find people who thought he was doing wonderful work. 'We are treated,' he says, 'as impostors, and yet are true'. He was treated 'as unknown, and yet well known'. There were those who wondered who on earth he was; yet he was well known to God, and well known to those who were God's. Hardest of all, he says, he has been treated 'as dying, and see—we are alive'. People thought they'd disposed of him. They stoned him. They thought they could kill him. Yet somehow he escaped them all.

And still there is more: '...as punished, and yet not killed'. He was always being thrown into jail, or beaten up, or punished in some way, either in the synagogue or by the civil authorities. 'As sorrowful, yet always rejoicing; as poor, yet making many rich, as having nothing and yet possessing everything.' These are the characteristic marks of the apostle. This is what made Paul who he was. Through it all he is saying, 'This is what it means to be a true servant of Christ, to be one in whose work the life, death and resurrection of Jesus Christ are presented to the world. We cannot merely talk about these things. What counts is doing them, living them out each day of our lives.'

When difficulties and dangers surround us, gracious Lord, enable us to trust you for everything, and continually to embody your own love and faithfulness. Amen.

WEEK 3 (SATURDAY)

2 CORINTHIANS 6:11–13

We have spoken frankly to you Corinthians; our heart is wide open to you. There is no restriction in our affections, but only in yours. In return— I speak as to children—open wide your hearts also.

Paul takes a deep breath and stands back from the whole passionate argument that he has been presenting. As best he can, while dictating a letter, he is trying to look his audience in the eye. He says: Listen, I have laid it on the line. I have bared my soul. I have worn my heart on my sleeve. I have spoken very frankly to you. I have not hidden from you anything that I have been feeling.

We are sometimes taught that it is embarrassing to wear our hearts on our sleeves. If we are sad, depressed or despondent, people will tell us that we should hide it, and pretend that all is well. Some people objected, on those grounds, to the outpouring of public grief for Diana, Princess of Wales. Paul certainly doesn't believe that. Our heart, he says, is wide open to you. (In the Greek he says, 'We have opened our mouth and our heart to you.') Nothing is hidden. There is no restriction (v. 12) in us, in our affections, so that any restriction in our relationship must be coming from your side.

Paul is facing his readers clearly with the fact that all has not been well. He has been in Ephesus, on the other side of the Aegean sea. They have been at home in Corinth, where teachers have come to them and belittled Paul. They have implied that he wasn't a real apostle, because he was always being thrown in jail, always getting on the wrong side of the law, and so on. So he says: any barrier between us has been put up from your side. I have been completely frank and honest with you. What would happen in Christian congregations today if clergy, and other people in positions of leadership, were always completely frank about how they felt, and about the relationship between themselves and the community? Many people would find that embarrassing, hard to take—and it is important to judge the appropriate moment for such frankness. But from time to time a moment comes when we need to say, 'All right, let's put everything on the table.'

And here Paul says: 'In return—I am speaking as to children—open wide your hearts also.' Often, when Paul is addressing people who have come to Christian faith through his own ministry, he thinks of himself and them in terms of parenthood. In Galatians 4:19 he talks about 'being in labour again' until his hearers have come to full birth. He speaks here as a father to children. He will not be a distant, detached authority figure; he has the right to appeal to them, because of the intimacy between them. He knows them through and through. And if they stop and think, they know him equally well. There is between them, in principle, that openness of relationship of which he spoke in chapter 3, in terms of the Spirit reflecting the glory of God. If they try to perceive the true nature of things, they will realize that they are reading the words of one in whom they see the glory of God at work.

This, then, is at the heart of Christian fellowship, and at the heart of the delicate and strange business of authority within the Christian community. It isn't a matter of one person barking orders at another, or a leader lording it over a group. Nor is it a matter of a majority vote on everything. It is a matter of somebody who has been entrusted with a ministry by God the Holy Spirit, and exercising that ministry in the knowledge that the same Spirit is at work in the congregation committed to their charge. If barriers arise in the midst of that, then ultimately all parties must take the risk of saying, 'There is nothing to be gained by hiding, nothing to be gained by pretending. Let us be frank in the Lord. Let us be honest and let us above all, individually, and in our relationships with one another, strive to reflect the open generosity of God, the glory of God revealed in Jesus Christ.'

God, after all, has spoken frankly to us in Jesus Christ, opening wide his heart. He does not restrict his affection towards us. If we find a barrier in our relationship with God, it is one that we have erected, not one that he has made. What Paul is giving in verses 11—13 is another example of how he actually expresses the generous love, the glory, of God. This divine glory is displayed not as a blinding light to dazzle us and leave us flat on our faces for ever in fear and trembling. It is the loving light of the gospel of the glory of God, revealed in Jesus Christ, opening our hearts to that glory, so that in receiving it, we ourselves can then be the bearers of it to a waiting world.

Enable us, Father, to be honest with you and with one another about our deepest and truest feelings. Amen.

WEEK 4 (SUNDAY)

COLOSSIANS 1:24–29

I am now rejoicing in my sufferings for your sake, and in my flesh I am completing what is lacking in Christ's afflictions for the sake of his body, that is, the church. I became its servant according to God's commission that was given to me for you, to make the word of God fully known, the mystery that has been hidden throughout the ages and generations but has now been revealed to his saints. To them God chose to make known how great among the Gentiles are the riches of the glory of this mystery, which is Christ in you, the hope of glory. It is he whom we proclaim, warning everyone and teaching everyone in all wisdom, so that we may present everyone mature in Christ. For this I toil and struggle with all the energy that he powerfully inspires within me.

As we move from looking at a long passage in 2 Corinthians towards the parts of John that we shall be examining as Lent draws to its climax in Holy Week, we have some New Testament passages which form a sort of bridge between the themes in each. The first of these is Colossians 1:24–29.

Here, as in 2 Corinthians, Paul explains to the young church in Colossae the nature of his ministry. He didn't found the church in Colossae. He didn't know them personally, apart from one or two people whom he may have met on his journeys. He is writing to encourage them in their new-found faith, and particularly to stir up in them the spirit of gratitude and thankfulness that he regards as such a central, key marker of Christian living.

He has just set out (1:15–20) the very basis and foundation of the Christian faith. Then, in 1:21–23, like someone who has drawn a map, he puts a marker on it saying, 'You are here'. The Colossian Christians belong in the middle of this map, the map of the world view that they have come to share. Now, in verses 24–29, he turns to describe his own work; and he begins with the extraordinary claim that he is rejoicing in his sufferings, which are on their behalf. Then, as though that weren't enough, he goes on to say, 'In my flesh I am completing what is lacking in Christ's afflictions for the sake of his body, that is, the church.'

Now we may well rub our eyes and stare at this. How can Paul say that there is something lacking in Christ's affliction? How can he be wanting to add to the finished work which Christ accomplished on the cross? The answer is that Paul isn't adding to it, but sharing it. This is how he sees his work, his whole vocation: that, as the apostle of Christ, he isn't somebody who simply talks about the sufferings of Christ. In his own life and struggle, he engages with the world in such a way that the life and struggle of Christ are re-embodied in him. And if he had been asked for further explanation, he would quickly have said that it came about through the work of the Holy Spirit, making Christ present in Paul himself.

So Paul understands his sufferings both by analogy with the sufferings of Christ, which are themselves on behalf of the church and the world, and also as participating in those Messianic sufferings. It is as if he, as the leader of the church in that part of the world (western Turkey, as we would call it today), is drawing the enemy fire on to himself, so that the young church may have a breathing space, time to grow. He is probably in prison in Ephesus when he is writing this letter, and he sees the powers of the world doing their worst to him. His response is, 'Well, as long as they are concentrating on me, then Christ's body, the church, can grow until it is strong enough to stand on its own feet.'

For this reason, he is rejoicing. He sees the outworking of the pattern of Christ, the pattern of suffering and glory and resurrection. This is what he means in verse 25, when he says that he became the servant of the church according to God's commission, in order to make the word of God fully known to the church. For Paul, 'making the word of God fully known' is never simply transferring intellectual ideas from one brain to another brain, from his mouth to people's ears. Rather, it is a matter of embodying the living and active word of God, the word which is a person, Jesus Christ.

Then Paul says, in verse 26, that this word of God is a 'mystery that has been hidden throughout the ages and generations but has now been revealed' to God's people, God's holy ones. This idea of a 'mystery' is something that may have been familiar to the Colossians in another context. There were many religions in ancient Turkey that we would loosely call 'mystery religions', in which some hidden secret was revealed to the initiates, supposedly giving them a new depth of spirituality. But God's mystery was not like that. It was not a private religion, but a secret plan that the creator of the universe had conceived, way, way back, and begun to implement by calling Abraham, Isaac and Jacob. He continued this plan through Moses, David and the prophets, and disclosed it, fully and gloriously, when he sent his son to die and rise again for the world.

This, Paul says, is the real secret of the universe, now revealed it to you, the people in Colossae: to you, and to all God's people, God has chosen 'to make known how great among the Gentiles are the riches of the glory of this mystery'. 'Among the Gentiles': the Colossians, who were formerly pagans, not Jews, had received the great blessing from the God of Israel! Yes, Paul says, this was part of the glory of it. Part of the mystery, the delicious secret, was that God had planned, as the creator of the world, to bless the whole world through Israel. And he would do so through the Jewish Messiah, the one who was called the Christ.

The heart of this mystery, this glorious, rich secret is 'Christ in you, the hope of glory'. What is that glory? Just this: that the Colossian Christians, a small group of people in a tiny little town a hundred miles from the sea in western Turkey, would become truly human beings. They would begin to reflect the image and glory of God. They would become the people God made them to be.

And how are they to become all this? Paul's answer is that the life of the Messiah himself is implanted in them by the Holy Spirit. Through him they are assured that this life will ultimately transform them, so that they become, as it were, younger brothers and sisters of the Messiah, little 'Christs' ('anointed ones') in their turn.

This Messiah, this Christ, is the person Paul proclaims (vv. 28–29). He warns them, teaches them, in all wisdom, in order to present them complete, mature, whole in Christ. The word 'complete' says it all. It is God's design that each one of his children should become fully what God intends them to be: mature human beings, mature Christians, complete within his purpose.

This, says Paul, is my aim. This is why I am toiling and struggling with all my energy. That might sound like the statement of a 'driven' person, a hopeless workaholic, but Paul has discovered that his energy does not come from his own resources. Just as the glory for the Colossians is 'Christ in them', so the glory for Paul is Christ in him, the one who inspires him, who gives him energy, and who works through him by his Spirit so that he can teach and live and suffer and rejoice with the Colossians. His longing is that they in turn, through learning who they are in Christ, and through learning to thank and praise God for that, can now impart their precious knowledge to the world around them.

Open our eyes, Father, that we may see and understand your secret plan, in Christ, to save your world; and so give us the energy to play our part in it. Amen.

WEEK 4 (MONDAY)

ROMANS 8:18–25

I consider that the sufferings of this present time are not worth comparing with the glory about to be revealed to us. For the creation waits with eager longing for the revealing of the children of God; for the creation was subjected to futility, not of its own will but by the will of the one who subjected it, in hope that the creation itself will be set free from its bondage to decay and will obtain the freedom of the glory of the children of God. We know that the whole creation has been groaning in labour pains until now; and not only the creation, but we ourselves, who have the first fruits of the Spirit, groan inwardly while we wait for adoption, the redemption of our bodies. For in hope we were saved. Now hope that is seen is not hope. For who hopes for what is seen? But if we hope for what we do not see, we wait for it with patience.

The twin themes of suffering and glory dominate one of Paul's greatest chapters. Here he draws together the threads of his greatest epistle, the letter to the Romans; almost every element in his thought is woven into this chapter at some point. At the heart of the chapter, in verses 18–25, Paul writes about the whole creation groaning, waiting, longing for the revealing of the children of God. Paul's own sufferings, which he mentions in verse 18, are just part of this greater suffering.

In Romans, above all his letters, Paul presents the full sweep of the purposes of God, from creation to new creation. It is all too easy to shrink our reading and our understanding of a text like this into terms simply of 'me and my salvation'. But for Paul it neither starts there nor finishes there. It starts with God the creator, revealing his power and glory in creation, and it ends with the entire created order set free from its present state of corruption and decay. The physicists tell us that one day our world will have cooled off and become uninhabitable, unfit for any kind of life. Paul would not disagree: the whole cosmos, he says, is at present

74

in bondage to decay. But that's not the end of the story. As God raised Jesus from the dead, so God will perform the same act of new creation for the whole world.

That is why Paul can say that the sufferings of this present time are not worth comparing with the glory that is to be revealed. At the present moment the world is in a state of groaning and suffering, and we ourselves, who are Christians, are in the same condition. There are many things which we long to be and do that, in our present state, we cannot hope to achieve. One day, though, when God gives us the renewed bodies that he has promised, we will be released to be and do all those things, just as he will renew the whole of creation.

Paul therefore speaks, in verse 19, of creation waiting eagerly. The picture this verb conjures up works like this: imagine somebody longing for a friend or a relative to come home. They stand at the door, straining their eyes, watching the road to see if there is any sight of this person returning. That, Paul says, is what the whole of creation is doing as it waits for the day when God's sons and daughters are revealed in their redeemed state. He adds in verse 20, '...the creation was subjected to futility, not of its own will, but by the will of the one who subjected it'. It was never God's intention that the world should be subjected to decay. God intended his creation to be the beginning of something glorious and ultimately permanent. Until we humans are made right with God, however, the creation, of which we are the flower, cannot be restored as God longs for it to be.

A day will surely come, says Paul in verse 21, when all creation will be set free. God will liberate his children, and thereby invite the whole creation to share in the party, to partake in 'the freedom of the glory of the children of God'. Paul here is deliberately echoing passages in scripture about the exodus of the children of Israel from Egypt. They were enslaved; God brought them out of Egypt; he led them through the wilderness, and home to their promised land, where they could worship him gladly and freely as he always wanted, and reveal his light and justice to the nations. At the resurrection God did for Jesus what he did for Israel, bringing him back from the bondage of death itself. He will now do for all his children, and ultimately for the whole creation, what he did for Jesus.

So, Paul declares in verses 22–23, we know that the whole creation has been groaning in travail until now. He uses the image of a mother giving birth, going through the pains of labour, to describe what is happening to the creation. We talk, casually perhaps, of 'nature, red in tooth and claw'. Paul sees beyond that, recognizing that creation is not yet all that God intends it to be. He looks for the time when the wolf will lie down with the lamb, and the cow and the bear will feed together, and a child will play at the cobra's den.

And we ourselves, who have the first fruits of the Spirit, are in the same attitude of waiting. God has already begun to work his glory within us. As a result, we realize that there is more in God's purpose for us than we have yet received. So we groan too. We groan inwardly while we wait for the redemption of our bodies, for it was in the hope of this that we were saved. As Paul puts it in Philippians 3:12, I haven't already attained this, I am not already perfect, 'but I press on to make it my own, because Christ Jesus has made me his own'. We don't hope for that which we already see. We hope for what we do not see, and wait for it with patience.

I love the picture of the church in this passage. We tend to think of the world getting itself into a hopeless mess, and the church going off and hiding in a building somewhere singing God's praises, pretending that all is well with them. That is not Paul's picture of the church. As we have already seen, his vision of the church, as of himself as the suffering apostle, is that it is called to be where the world is in pain, so that, by sharing the pain, it can be the means through which God himself, by the Spirit, is present even there.

We shouldn't, therefore, think that if the church finds itself in pain on some issue, some problem, some topic, this indicates that we have taken some terrible wrong turning. It might just be that we have been faithful to our vocation to groan inwardly because we have the first fruits of the Spirit. Our groaning takes up the groaning of all creation, and brings it mysteriously into the loving and healing presence of God. And if that is true for the church as a whole, it is certainly true for every individual Christian as well.

Give us courage and hope, Father, so that, as we share the groaning of all creation, we may know your presence with us and trust your promise of the final renewal of all things. Amen.

WEEK 4 (TUESDAY)

ROMANS 8:26–30

Likewise the Spirit helps us in our weakness; for we do not know how to pray as we ought, but that very Spirit intercedes with sighs too deep for words. And God, who searches the heart, knows what is the mind of the Spirit, because the Spirit intercedes for the saints according to the will of God.

We know that all things work together for good for those who love God, who are called according to his purpose. For those whom he foreknew he also predestined to be conformed to the image of his Son, in order that he might be the firstborn within a large family. And those whom he predestined he also called; and those whom he called he also justified; and those whom he justified he also glorified.

We saw yesterday that the church is called to share the pain of the world. What then is God doing in all this process? Is God simply sitting on the sidelines, looking on? No, according to verses 26 and 27. God, in the person of the Spirit, is groaning within the church.

Paul uses in verse 26 the same female image, that of groaning in labour pains, that he has used for the world in verse 22, and for the church in verse 23. The Spirit's own self groans within us with sighs too deep for words. Paul sees the prayer life of the church as the means by which God can come and share the pain of the world.

Many times individual Christians, and whole churches, feel that they don't really understand why they are in such pain, why they are facing such problems. Sometimes people find themselves in such a condition that they say they can't pray. They find it impossible to put into words the struggle and turmoil that they feel. At precisely that point, says Paul, the Spirit is groaning inarticulately within them. The good news (in verse 27) is that 'God, who searches the heart, knows what is the mind of the Spirit, because the Spirit intercedes for the saints according to the will of God.'

In this passage, we have God calling to God, and God answering God. God the Spirit, dwelling within the suffering church, is calling to God the Father, the creator. And the pattern that emerges as God the Father and God the Spirit engage in this strange conversation, this to-and-fro of groaning, listening, and answering, should be familiar to us. It is of course the pattern of Christ: bearing the pain of the world, caught between heaven and earth, belonging on earth and yet shot through with the life of heaven. The church is thus called, as Paul knows himself to be called, to be a company of people in whose experience the pain of God and the pain of the world are held together, so that the world may be redeemed.

Paul can then stand back from this, in verses 28–30, and sum up where the whole letter has reached at this point. 'We know,' he says, 'that all things work together for good for those who love God, who are called according to his purpose.' Christians can, too often, take this in a casual, almost flippant, fashion. 'Oh well,' someone says with a shrug, 'all things work together for good', as though that explained all the minor catastrophes and hazards of life. It is true that God knows about everything from the fall of the sparrow through to the great and often catastrophic events that happen to nations and kingdoms. But Paul has his eye on the cosmic future, on the revealing of the glory of God in and to the whole created order. He sees that all God's people are caught up in this wider activity and that through the achievement of Christ, and by the work of the Spirit, God will bring to completion the plan he established long ago.

Paul therefore invokes the language of God's calling of Israel, found in Deuteronomy, in Isaiah, and in many other Old Testament passages. That call has now broadened out, in Jesus the Jewish Messiah, to include not only Israel but also Gentiles. All those called in Christ to be God's people are assured that God's plan is going forward; and of course that plan is never for themselves alone. It is, through them, for the whole world, as we have already seen in verses 18–25. But Paul is writing to a struggling young church in Rome, faced with the might of the imperial capital on the one hand, and with a large unbelieving synagogue community on the other. The church, caught between these two, needs to know that God's purposes for his people are utterly secure. And so he says, 'Those whom he foreknew he also predestined to be conformed to the image of his Son, so that he might be the firstborn among many brothers and sisters.' This, however, raises other questions for us.

The central idea is that Christ is the older brother of the family of God. All those who belong to him will share his family likeness, his 'image'; they will become people in whom the glory of God is revealed to the world. God's intention to use them in this way means that he chose them beforehand, and then 'called' them. Paul uses the word 'call' to designate what happens when the gospel is proclaimed and people respond to it. Those who respond in faith are declared to be in truth members of God's family, even though the full revelation of the fact awaits the end of time: that is the meaning of 'justification by faith'.

Those whom God predestined he called; those whom he called, he justified; and, finally, those whom he justified he also glorified. That is to say, all those who are members of God's family are already glorified in Christ. God has given them the Spirit, so that the glory of God is dwelling within them. Paul, looking from the end of the process back to the beginning, can even use the past tense for something which is in fact still in the future, because it is so certain in the purposes of God. All those who believe the gospel of Jesus Christ are assured that they will one day fully reflect the glory of God, even as Christ reflects the glory of God. The sufferings of the present time—this is a Lent book, after all; we mustn't get too celebratory!—are not worth comparing with the glory that is to be revealed.

Pray with us and in us, Holy Spirit; that, being ourselves assured of your healing presence, we may bear the image of Christ into the world. Amen.

WEEK 4 (WEDNESDAY)

1 PETER 2:1–6

Rid yourselves, therefore, of all malice, and all guile, insincerity, envy, and all slander. Like newborn infants, long for the pure, spiritual milk, so that by it you may grow into salvation—if indeed you have tasted that the Lord is good.

Come to him, a living stone, though rejected by mortals yet chosen and precious in God's sight, and like living stones, let yourselves be built into a spiritual house, to be a holy priesthood, to offer spiritual sacrifices acceptable to God through Jesus Christ. For it stands in scripture: 'See, I am laying in Zion a stone, a cornerstone chosen and precious; and whoever believes in him will not be put to shame.'

Scholars are divided as to who wrote what we call the first letter of Peter, but we will call him Peter for the purpose of today's and tomorrow's readings. In this passage he paints a picture of the new temple for the young churches to whom he is writing.

The temple in Jerusalem was the very centre of the Jewish world view. It was the place where heaven and earth met, and the Jews didn't mean that metaphorically; they meant it quite literally. For them, heaven and earth were the two basic dimensions of God's creation, which co-existed unseen to one another. The place where they actually intersected and where you could virtually pass from one to the other was in the temple in Jerusalem. Once we appreciate this, we can see the significance of the way in which many New Testament writers, including Peter in this passage, pick up the image of the temple and apply it to the church. So here in verses 4–6 Peter talks about the church as a collection of stones being built into a spiritual house, a temple, where sacrifices are offered in fulfilment of the prophecy of scripture. And they are built on the foundation stone, which is Jesus himself.

As Peter wants to work up to that idea in verses 4–6 he begins the chapter with a warning, because any Jew coming up to the temple had to purify himself or herself so that they could enter joyfully into the service of God and offer the sacrifices gladly. So he says, there are certain things you have got to set aside as you approach the temple. This is a good theme for the halfway stage of Lent. 'Rid yourself of all malice, and all guile, insincerity, envy and all slander.' It is interesting that within the church we often focus on gross sins, on immorality or greed or whatever. But here we find things which are more subtle. Unfortunately, there are all too many churches where sexual immorality would be unthinkable but where these vices flourish and abound. And just as Paul in 2 Corinthians was insistent that the way of being a Christian is the way of being open-hearted, of speaking the truth frankly, of being quite clear before God and one another about our motives, so within the church it is vital that we lay aside all trickery, all deceit, if we are to be part of the living temple, offering spiritual sacrifices.

Instead, we are to come (v. 2) like little children, new-born infants, longing for the pure spiritual milk in order to grow up into full knowledge of salvation. Peter here draws on another Old Testament theme from Psalm 34: 'Taste and see that the Lord is good; happy are those who take refuge in him.' Once he has prepared people to shed what they must leave behind, and to thirst for the true spiritual milk, he invites them to come to the Lord, to Jesus himself, who is the living stone upon which the true temple is built.

This living stone, in fulfilment of scripture, was rejected by the official guardians of Israel's ancestral traditions, both by the chief priests and by the self-appointed law teachers, the Pharisees. They couldn't see that this was the way in which God's true temple was in fact to be built. And because of Jesus, Peter says, you must let yourselves be built like living stones 'into a spiritual house, to be a holy priesthood, to offer spiritual sacrifices acceptable to God through Christ'. Of course he is mixing his metaphors. You cannot be both the walls of the temple and the priesthood offering sacrifices inside. But we can see how each level of the metaphor works to make its own point. The temple was the dwelling-place of the living God. The church is now to be the place where he lives, because of the work of Jesus and the gift of the Holy Spirit. The priesthood consisted of those who offered sacrifices day by day in order to keep open the line of fellowship between God and Israel.

Likewise, the church is to be the community of people who offer what Peter here, and Paul in Romans 12, call 'spiritual sacrifices'.

Ultimately, of course, this means offering the whole of ourselves to God. It doesn't mean bribing God or twisting his arm. It means a glad self-offering, in response to God's grace, which is then made acceptable through Jesus Christ. Because God says (and here Peter quotes Isaiah 28, a passage which occurs in various other places in the New Testament), 'I am laying in Zion... a corner stone chosen and precious: and whoever believes in him [or in it] will not be put to shame'. In other words, here is the foundation stone, and you can trust your life to this foundation stone. If you build your whole life as an individual and particularly as a community on this stone, on Jesus himself, you will never find yourself put to shame.

This recalls that great image of house-building which runs right through the gospels from Jesus' parable about the wise man who built his house on the rock. The church is called to be the place where the living God makes his home, which means that the temple itself is made redundant. That is why in Revelation 21 there is no temple in the city—because God himself is present with his people. Peter points forward to that ultimate reality of the glory of God dwelling with his people, shining in and through them, so that they are his people and he is their God.

As we come to worship you, Father, give us cheerful courage to lay aside all that hinders us from entering your presence, so that we may be living stones, built into your new temple. Amen.

WEEK 4 (THURSDAY)

1 PETER 2:7–12

To you then who believe, he is precious; but for those who do not believe, 'The stone that the builders rejected has become the very head of the corner', and 'A stone that makes them stumble, and a rock that makes them fall.' They stumble because they disobey the word, as they were destined to do.

But you are a chosen race, a royal priesthood, a holy nation, God's own people, in order that you may proclaim the mighty acts of him who called you out of darkness into his marvellous light. Once you were not a people, but now you are God's people; once you had not received mercy, but now you have received mercy.

Beloved, I urge you as aliens and exiles to abstain from the desires of the flesh that wage war against the soul. Conduct yourselves honourably among the Gentiles, so that, though they malign you as evildoers, they may see your honourable deeds and glorify God when he comes to judge.

Peter now picks up the imagery from Isaiah that he has just quoted in verse 6, and insists first and foremost, 'To you then who believe, Jesus is precious.' The word 'precious' has been devalued in popular discourse, but within the original Greek it still carries the clear meaning of 'infinitely valuable'. It implies something which, if it were in a shop, would sit in the very centre of the window, an almost priceless piece of stock. Jesus is even more precious than that, yet he is given freely to all those who believe. But alas, as we see in the second half of verse 7 and in verse 8, there were those who in Peter's day had rejected him. In the words of scripture, he was the stone the builders rejected, who became 'the very head of the corner'. And Peter alludes to a theme we find worked out more fully in Paul's writings, that in the strange purposes of God, Jesus' contemporaries were bound to reject him. This rejection was the only way to save the world, the only way to make this new movement of God into a movement for the world rather than one confined to the Jewish people and their national aspirations.

In his writings, Paul emphasizes that the Jews are still just as welcome as anyone else within the people of God. There is no ultimate rejection of them. But here Peter is focusing on the contrast between those who refused to obey the gospel and those who have believed and obeyed the word of God in Jesus Christ. To these people (v. 9) are now assigned all those extraordinary Old Testament promises that we find in such passages as Exodus 19:5–6 and Isaiah 43. He is saying, in effect, *you* are the true Israel. *You* are the chosen race, the royal priesthood, the holy nation, God's own people. *You* are the people upon whom have devolved all the promises that God made to Israel. Again we should be careful to point out that the people to whom Peter is writing are not simply Gentile Christians. They are both Jewish and Gentile Christians—a whole new community created in the Jewish Messiah, Jesus, to be God's true Israel for the sake of the world.

He picks up on that last phrase at the end of verse 9. The reason you are so privileged is not so that you can sit back and enjoy your new status for its own sake. Rather, it is in order that you may 'proclaim the mighty acts of the one who called you out of darkness into his marvellous light'. In other words, if you are the chosen race, you are chosen in order that you can reveal God to the world. If you are the royal priesthood, you are priests so that you can offer the praises of creation before God. If you are the holy nation, you are the ones who are set apart for God's purposes in his world. If you are God's own people then you must embody God's love for the world, and proclaim his mighty acts. Because (v. 10, now quoting from the book of Hosea) 'Once you were not a people, but now you are God's people; once you had not received mercy, but now you have received mercy'. This passage describes how God was judging Israel but would then redeem her on the other side of judgment. And Peter insists that the people created by God in Christ are the people of God's own covenant, the bearers of his good news to the whole world.

How then are God's people to behave within the world? In verses 11 and 12, they are to behave not as conforming themselves to the standards that they find around them in society, but as travellers, going through the world without taking on the standards of the world. 'I urge you as aliens and exiles to abstain from the desires of the flesh that wage war against the soul.' Peter makes this plea not so much because they are to cultivate a private spirituality but because the soul is the place where the living God is present and active through them for the sake of the world. They would be disloyal to their vocation if they allowed the world to infect them with its darkness.

At the same time, though (v. 12), the pagans, among whom these new Christians are living, will sneer at them because they are threatened by the existence of this group who are passing through the world without owing it allegiance. Even though Christians may be maligned as evildoers, it is vital that they should behave with honour, truth and dignity before the world. Even though the people of the world abuse them, they will, in their heart of hearts, recognize these Christians as witnesses to a way of living that honours and glorifies God. On the day of judgment, those who looked on and sneered will finally realize their mistake. Others who encounter this new people of God in Jesus Christ, this people who are his temple, the chosen race, the royal priesthood, the holy nation, will find their eyes opened and will come themselves to glorify God.

Make us holy, gracious Lord, so that we can shine your light into the dark places of the world. Amen

WEEK 4 (FRIDAY)

REVELATION 4:1–11

After this I looked, and there in heaven a door stood open! And the first voice, which I had heard speaking to me like a trumpet, said, 'Come up here, and I will show you what must take place after this.' At once I was in the spirit, and there in heaven stood a throne, with one seated on the throne! And the one seated there looks like jasper and cornelian, and around the throne is a rainbow that looks like an emerald. Around the throne are twenty-four thrones, and seated on the thrones are twenty-four elders, dressed in white robes, with golden crowns on their heads. Coming from the throne are flashes of lightning, and rumblings and peals of thunder, and in front of the throne burn seven flaming torches, which are the seven spirits of God; and in front of the throne there is something like a sea of glass, like crystal.

Around the throne, and on each side of the throne, are four living creatures, full of eyes in front and behind: the first living creature like a lion, the second living creature like an ox, the third living creature with a face like a human face, and the fourth living creature like a flying eagle. And the four living creatures, each of them with six wings, are full of eyes all around and inside. Day and night without ceasing they sing, 'Holy, holy, holy, the Lord God the Almighty, who was and is and is to come.' And whenever the living creatures give glory and honour and thanks to the one who is seated on the throne, who lives for ever and ever, the twenty-four elders fall before the one who is seated on the throne and worship the one who lives for ever and ever; they cast their crowns before the throne, singing, 'You are worthy, our Lord and God, to receive glory and honour and power, for you created all things, and by your will they existed and were created.'

A couple of years ago, I was about to enter Lichfield Cathedral for a big service when one of my colleagues looked at the service, beamed, and said, 'I see we have one of the two most magnificent passages in the New Testament as our reading at this service.'

'What's that?' I asked. 'Revelation 4,' he replied. 'And the other?' 'Revelation 5, of course!' was his reply. We are going to look at these two passages as a link between the themes we have been following in the writings of Paul and Peter across to the world of John's Gospel. In Revelation 4 and 5 we have a picture of worship—the whole of creation at worship.

This is not a picture of the far-off future. People are sometimes put off by verse 1, which says, 'I will show you what must take place after this.' Revelation 4 and 5 are not a revelation of what will take place in the future. Rather, they show the worship which goes on continually before the throne of God night and day; and that is the context in which the vision of the future is granted. In his vision John sees God on the throne (vv. 2 and 3), and around the throne twenty-four elders on twenty-four thrones. This presumably represents Israel and the church, the twelve and the twelve, worshipping God eternally.

And the truth of this vision is that what goes on in the heavenly realm is the counterpart of the worship going on in the earthly realm. Throughout the Bible, but particularly in Revelation, heaven and earth are not separate in the sense of heaven being solely in the future and earth in the present, or heaven being ten miles up in the air and earth being down here where we live. Heaven and earth are the two dimensions of God's whole reality, as we have seen in the other readings. What we are invited to understand is that when the church, the people of God, are worshipping God on earth, the heavenly reality is this wonderful scene of God on the throne surrounded by the elders worshipping him, accompanied by flashes of lighting and peals of thunder and all the other accoutrements of the magnificence and glory of God.

Around the throne are four living creatures, a picture drawn partly from the book of Ezekiel and partly from other stock Jewish images. They look like a lion, an ox, a creature with a human face, and an eagle. The church in the second and subsequent centuries would see these living creatures as images of the four evangelists, Matthew, Mark, Luke and John, but there is no hint of that here. These living creatures represent the world of creation as a whole, and that world of creation is also worshipping God. We are invited, then, to see in this glorious picture not just some human beings choosing to worship God, but the whole creation—the animals, the trees, the rivers, the sea, the sky—also worshipping by being truly themselves. When the penguins are sliding over the ice, when the trees are putting forth their green shoots in the spring, when clouds pass across the sky, they are being themselves to the glory of God.

In verse 8 we find that the song sung by creation, by the four living creatures, is simply expressive of the glory of God: 'Holy, holy, holy, the Lord God Almighty, who was and is and is to come.'

But then when the twenty-four elders cast their crowns before the throne, their song is different from the song creation sings. They are praising God as well, but they understand *why* they are praising God. 'You are worthy, our Lord and God, to receive glory and honour and power, because you created all things, and by your will they existed and were created.'

Here then is the picture in Revelation 4 of the worship of all creation. The church, the people of God, understands that God is the creator, understands that as such he is a glorious God, full of extraordinary ideas and inventive imagination. We just have to think for two minutes about the world of creation and imagine the same God creating a giraffe and creating a strawberry, the same God creating a waterfall and creating the look of delight on a new-born baby's face. God is full of extraordinary riches, and while the rest of creation worships God by simply being as it is, human beings are designed to draw out the praises of creation and, by understanding, to express that praise to God, giving God intelligent worship. As a result, we see in Revelation 4 a picture of the church poised between creation and new creation. We are the people who draw out the praises of creation, understand them, and lay them before the throne of God in gladness. And we are the people who thereby point to what we shall see in the next chapter, the new creation that God has in mind, his plan, for his people and for the universe as a whole.

Help us, Father, so to understand and appreciate what you have given us in your creation that we may worship you with mind as well as heart. Amen.

WEEK 4 (SATURDAY)

REVELATION 5:1–14

Then I saw in the right hand of the one seated on the throne a scroll written on the inside and on the back, sealed with seven seals; and I saw a mighty angel proclaiming with a loud voice, 'Who is worthy to open the scroll and break its seals?' And no one in heaven or on earth or under the earth was able to open the scroll or to look into it. And I began to weep bitterly because no one was found worthy to open the scroll or to look into it. Then one of the elders said to me, 'Do not weep. See, the Lion of the tribe of Judah, the Root of David, has conquered, so that he can open the scroll and its seven seals.'

Then I saw between the throne and the four living creatures and among the elders a Lamb standing as if it had been slaughtered, having seven horns and seven eyes, which are the seven spirits of God sent out into all the earth. He went and took the scroll from the right hand of the one who was seated on the throne. When he had taken the scroll, the four living creatures and the twenty-four elders fell before the Lamb, each holding a harp and golden bowls full of incense, which are the prayers of the saints. They sing a new song: 'You are worthy to take the scroll and to open its seals, for you were slaughtered and by your blood you ransomed for God saints from every tribe and language and people and nation; you have made them to be a kingdom and priests serving our God, and they will reign on earth.'

Then I looked, and I heard the voice of many angels surrounding the throne and the living creatures and the elders; they numbered myriads of myriads and thousands of thousands, singing with full voice, 'Worthy is the Lamb that was slaughtered to receive power and wealth and wisdom and might and honour and glory and blessing!'

Then I heard every creature in heaven and on earth and under the earth and in the sea, and all that is in them, singing, 'To the one seated on the throne and to the Lamb be blessing and honour and glory and might for ever and ever!' And the four living creatures said, 'Amen!' And the elders fell down and worshipped.

Within God's good creation there is an apparent problem. When God made the world, in Genesis 1 and 2, it wasn't simply static, like a painting on canvas, very beautiful but with no room for change or development. God wanted it to develop; he wanted human beings to bring order and beauty into his world. He wanted them to be his wise stewards over creation. What happened, of course, is that the human race turned away from God in ways that are difficult to describe but very clear in their effects to this day, in our own lives and in the world. God's purpose, the purpose for which he made the world, has yet to be put into effect. God has (in the language of this vision) a scroll, but it is sealed with seven seals. The scroll, which is God's future design and desire for the world, is at present sealed up. And no one (v. 3) in heaven or on earth or under the earth is able to open the scroll and look into it.

It looks as though creation is going to be frustrated. God himself will be frustrated. What will happen to his plan for the world? As John the seer looks on, he weeps bitterly because God's creation seems doomed to final failure. But (v. 5) one of the elders comforts him: 'Do not weep. See, the lion of the tribe of Judah, the Root of David, has conquered.' This is an image taken from many Jewish pictures of the Messiah, the coming king who would fulfil God's purpose for his chosen people. He now has the right to open the seven seals of the scroll.

And then, in one of the many kaleidoscopic changes of imagery in Revelation, we strain to glimpse the lion, but what we see is the lamb. Between the throne and the four living creatures and among the elders is a lamb, looking as if it had been slaughtered. It is one of the strangest of pictures—a lion who is also a lamb, who has been killed but is now alive. Somehow John wants us to hold that extraordinary combination of images in our heads and also to imagine that this lamb has seven horns and seven eyes, which are the seven spirits of God sent out into all the earth. Jesus Christ the king, the Lord, has achieved God's purpose for his world, and as a result is now the one through whom God's Spirit is sent out to implement his achievement in all the world.

He takes the scroll from the one who sits on the throne and now, because he is the Lord of history, the living creatures and the twenty-four elders sing a new song (v. 9): 'You are worthy to take the scroll and open the seals because you were slaughtered, and by your blood you ransomed for God [people to be] saints from every tribe and language and nation; you have made them to be kings and priests, serving God, and they will reign on the earth.' In other words, because of what the Lamb has achieved in his obedient death and resurrection, there is now a new company of people, represented by the twenty-four elders, who are a royal priesthood, a holy nation. This again picks up the theme of Exodus, echoing what Peter said about the church being God's agents to effect his purpose in the world. And then, as a result of the work of the Lamb, and as a result of the coming into being of this people, the whole creation sings this new song, with angels joining in: 'Worthy is the Lamb that was slaughtered to receive power and wealth and wisdom and might and honour and glory and blessing!' And the whole creation joins in the song: 'To the one seated on the throne, be blessing and honour, glory and might, for ever and ever. Amen.'

In this extraordinary vision, full of glory and worship, we find the church revealed as the true Israel. This is the vision that should inform the Christian's calling to worship, that when we worship God—whether alone in a room, in a small church service with half a dozen people, in a huge celebration with thousands crammed into a stadium to worship God, or in a march going on all around the world, with millions of people joining in—it is all part of the heavenly reality. Our praises join with those eternal songs going on day by day, night by night. The church is poised between Israel and new creation, between the old creation and the consummation of all things in Christ. Our worship is to be worship of the God we see revealed in Jesus, the God who has revealed his glory supremely in the death and resurrection of Jesus. It is because this God has thus shown us his glory, shown us who he is, that we in our worship can use both hearts and minds in praise. We can intelligently, lovingly, and with great celebration, declare to the one seated on the throne and to the lamb, all blessing and honour and glory and might for ever and ever. Amen.

As we glimpse your purpose, Father, revealed through the lion who is also the lamb, we pray that we may also realize that our small worship forms part of the great song of praise from all your people living and departed, and so be strengthened in our faith and joy. Amen.

WEEK 5 (SUNDAY)

JOHN 1:1–18

In the beginning was the Word, and the Word was with God, and the Word was God. He was in the beginning with God. All things came into being through him, and without him not one thing came into being. What has come into being in him was life, and the life was the light of all people. The light shines in the darkness, and the darkness did not overcome it.

There was a man sent from God, whose name was John. He came as a witness to testify to the light, so that all might believe through him. He himself was not the light, but he came to testify to the light. The true light, which enlightens everyone, was coming into the world.

He was in the world, and the world came into being through him; yet the world did not know him. He came to what was his own, and his own people did not accept him. But to all who received him, who believed in his name, he gave power to become children of God, who were born, not of blood or of the will of the flesh or of the will of man, but of God.

And the Word became flesh and lived among us, and we have seen his glory, the glory as of a father's only son, full of grace and truth. (John testified to him and cried out, 'This was he of whom I said, "He who comes after me ranks ahead of me because he was before me." ') From his fullness we have all received, grace upon grace. The law indeed was given through Moses; grace and truth came through Jesus Christ. No one has ever seen God. It is God the only Son, who is close to the Father's heart, who has made him known.

'In the beginning was the Word.' I suspect there are many people in England who, if they know no other sentences in the New Testament, know that one—because they have heard it in carol services, in parish churches, or on the radio, every Christmas. Very few perhaps realize what John is doing when he starts his Gospel with those words.

Any Jew or Christian in the first century would know that if somebody starts a book with the words 'in the beginning' he is saying as clearly as he can, 'This is a new genesis, a new beginning.' 'In the beginning God created the heavens and the earth.' And now, 'In the beginning was the Word.' It is as though somebody started a new symphony today with the first four notes of Beethoven's Fifth Symphony. We would know at once that he was quoting and making a statement about the subject matter of his symphony.

What then does it mean when we say that this passage is a new genesis? It is a story of creation, but told here with Jesus in the middle of it, Jesus as the Word of God. The Jewish people had various ways of talking about how their God, the creator of the world, was not distant or detached from the world. While remaining distinct from the world, he was active still within the world. They spoke of God's spirit or breath, his *shekinah* or glorious presence in the temple. They spoke of God's law, the perfect law that he had given to Moses as the pattern of life for his people. They spoke of God's wisdom, the means by which he made the world, and which was now given to human beings so that they too could be wise. And again and again they spoke of God's word. So there were five ways in which they spoke of God as present, loving, living, powerful and active within the world that he had made: Spirit or breath, *Shekinah*, Law, Wisdom and Word.

John in this passage picks up the concept of the Word to express his firmly held belief that in Jesus of Nazareth he had seen and heard the one who was the perfect self-expression of God. And because he is also thinking of all those other ways in which God is active within the world, he describes Jesus in language taken from Jewish poems about the Wisdom of God, through whom God made the world and who actually comes to dwell with God's people.

At the climax of this passage (John 1:1–18) he speaks of the Word becoming flesh and living among us. The word for 'lived' is a word meaning 'pitched his tent', 'came to dwell', as God came to dwell in the temple when the cloud of his glory, the *shekinah*, came down. So this Jesus, this Word of God, this Wisdom of God, is also the *Shekinah*, the means by which God enters the temple to be with his people.

As we shall see, this is one of the great themes of John's Gospel: Jesus coming to the temple, Jesus enacting in the sight of

Israel and even the world the true role of the temple. We will find later on in the Gospel that Jesus is the one through whom God gives the Spirit to the church and to the world, and John highlights this towards the end of our present passage (v. 17): 'The law indeed was given through Moses; grace and truth came through Jesus Christ.' Jesus is the one who fulfils all that God had done through the law of Moses. In the prologue to his Gospel, John has said, as clearly as any first-century Jew could, that in Jesus of Nazareth the one true God—the God of Israel—has revealed himself. The revelation is not only to people's minds, giving them an intellectual idea of who he was, but to their hearts, giving his own self, his own presence. And above all, in this Gospel of John, we learn how God has given his love and his glory to his people, to be with them, to be for them, to be lived out through them.

John goes on in this passage to pile up themes which he will explore throughout the rest of the Gospel, themes we shall consider as we study some key passages in the rest of this Lent. Among these themes are the life which was in God and in Christ, and which has now been given to the world; the light, which was the light of Christ shining in the darkness, the light of the world which has come to God's people so that they can shine in turn; and the coming of God into a world which does not recognize him, and to a people that does not recognize him.

Then comes verse 12: 'To all who received him [Jew and Gentile alike, as we shall see in John chapter 12], who believed in his name, he gave power to become children of God.' And just as the book of Genesis begins with the making of the world, with the crown of creation being the shaping of man and woman in God's image, so this extraordinary poem of new creation in John 1:1–18 reaches its climax with that wonderful statement in verse 14: 'the Word became flesh'. How else could the living God express himself within the world? What else would he become if not a human being, made in his image? John goes on to say that we have seen his glory, the glory as of a Father's only Son, the perfect reflection of the glory of God.

As we continue to read through the Gospel, we shall see that, for John, this glory was revealed not in a blaze of majesty, not in Jesus' sweeping all before him in some triumphal earthly procession. This glory was revealed supremely in Jesus' giving of his own life as the sacrifice for the sins of the world, enthroned on the cross outside Jerusalem and crowned with cruel thorns. It is in the light of that knowledge that John writes verse 18: 'No one has ever seen God. It is God the only Son, who is close to the Father's heart, who has made him known.' In other words, when we look at this Jesus, and above all at Jesus crucified for the sins of the world, then we see the true nature of the Father's heart. It is a heart of glory, the glory of self-giving love.

Word incarnate, visible Son of the invisible Father; open our minds to your truth, our eyes to your light, and our hearts to your grace. Amen.

WEEK 5 (MONDAY)

JOHN 7:37–39

On the last day of the festival, the great day, while Jesus was standing there, he cried out, 'Let anyone who is thirsty come to me, and let the one who believes in me drink. As the scripture has said, "Out of the believer's heart shall flow rivers of living water."' Now he said this about the Spirit, which believers in him were to receive; for as yet there was no Spirit, because Jesus was not yet glorified.

Jesus has come to Jerusalem for the Feast of Tabernacles. This is one of the great Jewish festivals, in part commemorating one of the episodes during the Israelites' wilderness wanderings, led by the strange grace of God after their escape from Egypt. The story commemorated in the Feast is recorded in the book of Exodus; the people were thirsty and God quenched their thirst when Moses struck a rock and water flowed from it. In some Jewish traditions the rock that Moses had struck then followed the people around in the wilderness, so that there was always more water whenever they needed it. This was one of the delightful rabbinic ways of describing graphically how God provided for his people in the desert. That image of water flowing out to refresh parched ground and to refresh thirsty people remains one of the central images in Jewish life and expectation. If you have ever been to the Middle East you will know that if you spend half an hour in the desert you certainly need water.

On the eighth and last day of this festival, Jesus stood up in the temple and shouted, 'Let anyone who is thirsty come to me, and let the one who believes in me drink.' He was here alluding to Isaiah 55: the prophet calls out to the people that any who are hungry or thirsty should come to the waters, come and buy wine and have a great feast, even if they have no money. God's people were invited to the festival banquet that God would provide for all his people.

And now Jesus is saying: I am going to do it. I am the one through whom all God's promises will be fulfilled. If you follow me, you will experience a new exodus. If you follow me, you too will find a rock in the wilderness that supplies you with fresh water.

Then the image changes, because it implies more than people satisfying their own thirst. It implies that ordinary people can become the means by which God satisfies the thirst of others. John draws on a temple image found at the end of the book of Ezekiel, in that strange, dream-like passage (chs. 40–47) that gives a picture of the renewed temple. Ezekiel was a priest as well as a prophet, and he had mourned the Babylonian destruction of the temple and above all the fact that God had abandoned the temple because of the sin of the people. In Ezekiel chapters 34–37, however, the prophet declares that God will restore the fortunes of his people, cleansing them and giving them a new spirit, raising them from their graves in Babylon and bringing them home to their own land. And God will make a new temple in Jerusalem, and out of this temple will flow a river of living water, which meant running water as opposed to stagnant water in a cistern or a lake. This living water will flow out to irrigate the parched desert, even down to the Dead Sea. The rivers of living water will make the Dead Sea fresh, and people will stand and fish on the banks.

Jesus refers here to this image of living water as a great picture of the new covenant that God will make with his people for all the world. In verse 38, he says: if you believe in me and drink the water that I will give, then, as the scripture said, out of your heart shall flow rivers of living water. Now there is no passage in the Jewish scriptures that uses those precise words. It seems as though Jesus is taking a temple theme—after all, he was standing there in the temple at Jerusalem—and saying that all who believed in him would become a source of life, just like the new temple. Through their life and work and witness, God would irrigate the dry and barren world all around.

John comments in verse 39 that Jesus was referring to the Spirit, which believers in him were to receive, for as yet the Spirit had not been given. The Greek, indeed, is stronger than that, and says, 'There was not yet the Spirit, because Jesus was not yet glorified.' John is pointing here to the events immediately after the resurrection of Jesus, in chapter 20, when the risen Lord greets his followers with the words, 'As the Father has sent me, so I send you.' To equip them for this remarkable commission, he continues by breathing on them, and saying, 'Receive the Holy Spirit. If you forgive the sins of any, they are forgiven them; if you retain the sins of any, they are retained.' In other words, it is only when Jesus is glorified, that is, lifted up on the cross to bear the sins of the world, that the Spirit of God can be poured out upon his people. Through the cross they have been made fit to receive it, not only for themselves, but for all the parched and desert areas of the world, making even the Dead Sea fresh.

This gives us, then, a window not only on Jesus' vocation, but on our own vocation. We must come to Jesus to drink of the living water, not only to satisfy our own thirst but so that we can be the people through whom God restores the barren and broken land all around us.

Refresh us, gracious Lord, with living water, that from our hearts too that water may flow out to the world that needs it so badly. Amen.

WEEK 5 (TUESDAY)

JOHN 9:1–12

As he walked along, he saw a man blind from birth. His disciples asked him, 'Rabbi, who sinned, this man or his parents, that he was born blind?' Jesus answered, 'Neither this man nor his parents sinned; he was born blind so that God's works might be revealed in him. We must work the works of him who sent me while it is day; night is coming when no one can work. As long as I am in the world, I am the light of the world.' When he had said this, he spat on the ground and made mud with the saliva and spread the mud on the man's eyes, saying to him, 'Go, wash in the pool of Siloam' (which means Sent). Then he went and washed and came back able to see. The neighbours and those who had seen him before as a beggar began to ask, 'Is this not the man who used to sit and beg?' Some were saying, 'It is he.' Others were saying, 'No, but it is someone like him.' He kept saying, 'I am the man.' But they kept asking him, 'Then how were your eyes opened?' He answered, 'The man called Jesus made mud, spread it on my eyes, and said to me, "Go to Siloam and wash." Then I went and washed and received my sight.' They said to him, 'Where is he?' He said, 'I do not know.'

In the chapter immediately before today's passage, Jesus proclaims that he is the light of the world. Whoever follows him will never walk in darkness, but will have the light of life. This begins a lengthy discussion with the Pharisees and others, who were puzzled and indeed angry that Jesus should make such claims for himself. But then in chapter 9 Jesus does something to show what he meant by that claim. We should not assume that when Jesus declared himself the light of the world he was claiming to be the second person of the Trinity, or the divine incarnate Son of God. Of course, John intends us to hear all those levels of meaning as well, but, for Jesus' hearers, being the light of the world was first and foremost the task of Israel.

Israel was the light to the nations, the servant of the Lord, the people through whom God would shine upon the world; but Jesus is claiming that Israel's destiny is being fulfilled in himself. Indeed, if we look around the world of the first century, we find plenty of other groups who claimed exactly the same thing. There were messianic groups whose leaders claimed that their movement, their particular way of trying to be the people of God, was the fulfilment of all God's plans for Israel. Jesus knew that there were other would-be messiahs around, but he was different. He wasn't simply calling people to join a great revolution. He was finding people in desperate need and bringing God's love to them, vividly and personally.

In this story of the man who had been blind from birth we find Jesus bringing the light of the world to somebody who had never seen light at all. Jesus' disciples are clearly muddled about how such a thing can be, because in verse 2 they say, in effect, 'We presume that if he was born blind it must be because either he had sinned or his parents had sinned.' Jesus disagrees, telling them that it is more mysterious, less straightforward than that. God's works, his glory, are going to be revealed in this man, and Jesus reminds his followers that 'we must work the works of him who sent me while it is day; night is coming when no one can work.' Perhaps he was looking ahead to the time when he would be taken from them and crucified, when for a moment it would seem that the whole plan of God had come to a standstill. But he goes on to say in verse 5, 'As long as I am in the world, I am the light of the world.'

Jesus, then, quite clearly claims that his mission is the fulfilment of all that God has promised to do through Israel. But he does more than claim it, he enacts it. He makes some mud with his spittle on the ground (v. 6), spreads the mud on the man's eyes, and tells him to go and wash in the Pool of Siloam. The man goes, and washes, and comes back able to see. Some people watching this incident might have had a dim memory of the prophet Elisha telling Naaman the Syrian to go and wash in the Jordan. When Naaman had sufficient faith to do that, after grumbling and refusing to go, he came back cleansed of his leprosy. The blind man, too, had sufficient faith to do what he was told, and he returned, seeing.

There follows, as is usual in John, a little conversation between those who are puzzled and those who understand, those who don't believe it and the man himself in the middle of the controversy, who says: yes, this is me, this is what's happened to me.

In verse 11 he explains how Jesus made mud, put it on his eyes, and told him to go and wash. 'Then I went and washed and received my sight.' In the next verse, the people ask where Jesus has gone, but the man does not know. This, I think, is a typical way in which John points beyond an incident to show that even when Jesus was at work healing people, being the light of the world, they were looking and looking but still not seeing. They were trying to understand what was going on, but failing to get the message. There were some who pierced the disguise and believed, but, as John says in his Prologue, he came even to his own, and his own did not receive him.

John then launches us into a long discussion between the Pharisees and Jesus about what it means to open the eyes of the blind, what it means to be the light of the world. When we put this together with the rest of John's Gospel, we discover that the picture taking shape is not only of Jesus as the light of the world but of those whose spiritual blindness is healed becoming in turn the light of the world. Even by the end of this chapter the man whose eyes have been opened starts to bear witness to Jesus. 'One thing I do know, that though I was blind, now I see.'

He refuses to retract that basic testimony, even though the Jewish leaders then declare that as Jesus is to be shunned so this man should be shunned. He prefers to be shunned with Jesus than to cling to security by denying Jesus. The task of those whose eyes are opened by Jesus is not necessarily to understand it all, not necessarily to grasp all the finer points. They must simply bear witness to what Jesus has done for them, so that they are, in turn, lights of the world.

Enable us, O Lord our healer, to bear witness to what you have done for us, even when it is not what people want to hear. Amen.

WEEK 5 (WEDNESDAY)

JOHN 10:1–18

'Very truly, I tell you, anyone who does not enter the sheepfold by the gate but climbs in by another way is a thief and a bandit. The one who enters by the gate is the shepherd of the sheep. The gatekeeper opens the gate for him, and the sheep hear his voice. He calls his own sheep by name and leads them out. When he has brought out all his own, he goes ahead of them, and the sheep follow him because they know his voice. They will not follow a stranger, but they will run from him because they do not know the voice of strangers.' Jesus used this figure of speech with them, but they did not understand what he was saying to them.

So again Jesus said to them, 'Very truly, I tell you, I am the gate for the sheep. All who came before me are thieves and bandits; but the sheep did not listen to them. I am the gate. Whoever enters by me will be saved, and will come in and go out and find pasture. The thief comes only to steal and kill and destroy. I came that they may have life, and have it abundantly.

'I am the good shepherd. The good shepherd lays down his life for the sheep. The hired hand, who is not the shepherd and does not own the sheep, sees the wolf coming and leaves the sheep and runs away—and the wolf snatches them and scatters them. The hired hand runs away because a hired hand does not care for the sheep. I am the good shepherd. I know my own and my own know me, just as the Father knows me and I know the Father. And I lay down my life for the sheep. I have other sheep that do not belong to this fold. I must bring them also, and they will listen to my voice. So there will be one flock, one shepherd. For this reason the Father loves me, because I lay down my life in order to take it up again. No one takes it from me, but I lay it down of my own accord. I have power to lay it down, and I have power to take it up again. I have received this command from my Father.'

One of the most common images of God in the Old Testament is that of a shepherd: 'The Lord is my shepherd, I shall not want'

(Psalm 23). Ezekiel chapter 34 describes Israel in exile as like sheep who have been scattered because their shepherds have failed to do their job, looking after themselves rather than feeding the sheep. God declares that he will come to be the shepherd of his people: gathering up the lame, rescuing the stragglers, binding the injured and leaving the healthy and strong to play (I particularly like that bit!). And a little later in the vision, just as we might be wondering how God proposes to do this remarkable thing, he announces through the prophet (v. 23) that David his servant would be the shepherd. In other words, God will send a messiah, a king, who will do this work for God, serving as the true shepherd of the people.

When we turn to John 10, we find Jesus using this image of the true shepherd; his hearers would immediately think that he was comparing himself to David. David was the shepherd king, who knew how to rescue sheep from lions and bears, but who was taken from the pasture to be king of God's people Israel. And Jesus' audience would also think of the new David, the Messiah, sent by God to be the shepherd of all his people.

Using this language of sheep and shepherd, Jesus presents three different images. In the first six verses of the chapter, he talks about those who come and go out by the gate of the sheepfold, but warns of strangers who will try to climb in by another way—the thieves and bandits. One of the words he uses to refer to these strangers means far more than somebody who steals another's property. It was used in the first century for the revolutionaries, the other sorts of messianic leaders who would come and try to lead God's people in violent uprising. These uprisings, as Jesus knew, always ended with thousands of people being killed by the authorities, with crosses erected not only on one hillside but all over the place. In contrast, Jesus sees himself as the true shepherd who has come to lead God's people in a revolution of love that will change not only Israel but the whole world.

Jesus goes on to say (vv. 4–5) that when the true shepherd calls, his sheep will know him by his voice and come. Jesus is warning the people in Jerusalem that if they find that they understand what he is saying, they must follow him. Then they will find he leads them in the way that God intends Israel to go. In verse 6, however, John says that the people did not understand what he was saying to them, so Jesus develops a fresh, remarkable image.

A century or so ago, a scholar was wandering in Palestine, talking to local people about their way of life. One day he spoke to a shepherd, asking him how he kept the sheep safe at night. The shepherd described how he would bring the sheep into the sheepfold and then, when they were safely inside, he would lie down at the entrance. And this simple Palestinian said to the scholar, in Arabic, 'I am the door.' The scholar nearly dropped his pen in surprise, because he knew—though the shepherd didn't— that this was precisely what Jesus said in verse 9 of John chapter 10: 'I am the door, I am the gate.' The shepherd himself becomes the door protecting the sheep, keeping thieves, bandits or wolves at bay. Anyone who comes in and out through this doorway, under the eye of the shepherd, will be safe. The thief (v. 10) comes only to steal and kill and destroy, but Jesus comes as the good shepherd, so that his sheep can have life, abundant life. So we have here a picture of Jesus and Israel, Jesus as the Messiah who is charged with looking after the people of God and leading them to safety in a way that the bandits, the thieves, the revolutionaries could never have done.

The third image comes in verses 11 to 18, where Jesus says plainly, 'I am the true shepherd, the good shepherd. I am the shepherd for whom you have been waiting, the one who will lay down his life for the sheep.' And at this moment his words point ahead to the death that he would die. If he was no more than a hired hand he would have run away at the first whiff of danger, leaving the sheep scattered and vulnerable. This is another reference back to Ezekiel, to the false shepherds who do not care for the people. Jesus might also have had in mind some of the religious groups of his time—the Pharisees, for example, who were actually leading Israel astray in Jesus' eyes. He might also have been thinking of the chief priests, who were regularly in league with the Romans rather than looking after God's people. But 'I am the good shepherd,' he says; 'I know my own and my own know me.'

Turning to verse 15, we discover that, just as in Ezekiel 34, Jesus as the Messiah is allowing God to work through him, creating between God and his people the intimacy that already exists between Heavenly Father and Son: 'I know my own and my own know me, just as the Father knows me and I know the Father.' And how can Jesus truly express the Father God's love and care for his people? He will lay down his life for the sheep. This is the focus, the central part of his work as the living embodiment of the Father's love. God so loved the world that he gave his only Son.

In verse 16 there is the reminder that the Father is the creator of the world, not just of Israel, and so there are other sheep who must come. They do not yet belong to this fold, the fold of Israel, but Jesus will bring them also. They will listen to his voice, and in the end there will be one flock under one shepherd, a flock composed of people of all nations and kindreds and tribes and tongues. This is the command, the mission that he has received from the Father. Through the familiar, comforting image of a shepherd, Jesus tells how the story of Israel comes to its fulfilment. He knows, as he speaks, that this fulfilment will be achieved only through his death, the death by which he will glorify God, allowing God's love to be poured out upon the world. And he leaves his listeners with a hint of how the story of the whole world will reach a new climax, when Jew and Gentile alike are united into the single family of God, redeemed by the good shepherd.

Gather us, Good Shepherd, into one flock, hearing your voice, obeying your call, and led by you to safety. Amen.

WEEK 5 (THURSDAY)

JOHN 11:17–44

When Jesus arrived, he found that Lazarus had already been in the tomb for four days. Now Bethany was near Jerusalem, some two miles away, and many of the Jews had come to Martha and Mary to console them about their brother. When Martha heard that Jesus was coming, she went and met him, while Mary stayed at home. Martha said to Jesus, 'Lord, if you had been here, my brother would not have died. But even now I know that God will give you whatever you ask of him.' Jesus said to her, 'Your brother will rise again.' Martha said to him, 'I know that he will rise again in the resurrection on the last day.' Jesus said to her, 'I am the resurrection and the life. Those who believe in me, even though they die, will live, and everyone who lives and believes in me will never die. Do you believe this?' She said to him, 'Yes, Lord, I believe that you are the Messiah, the Son of God, the one coming into the world.'

When she had said this, she went back and called her sister Mary, and told her privately, 'The Teacher is here and is calling for you.' And when she heard it, she got up quickly and went to him. Now Jesus had not yet come to the village, but was still at the place where Martha had met him. The Jews who were with her in the house, consoling her, saw Mary get up quickly and go out. They followed her because they thought that she was going to the tomb to weep there. When Mary came where Jesus was and saw him, she knelt at his feet and said to him, 'Lord, if you had been here, my brother would not have died.' When Jesus saw her weeping, and the Jews who came with her also weeping, he was greatly disturbed in spirit and deeply moved. He said, 'Where have you laid him?' They said to him, 'Lord, come and see.' Jesus began to weep. So the Jews said, 'See how he loved him!' But some of them said, 'Could not he who opened the eyes of the blind man have kept this man from dying?'

Then Jesus, again greatly disturbed, came to the tomb. It was a cave, and a stone was lying against it. Jesus said, 'Take away the stone.' Martha, the sister of the dead man, said to him, 'Lord, already there is a stench because he has been dead for four days.' Jesus said to her, 'Did I not tell you that if you believed, you would see the glory of God?' So they took away the stone. And Jesus looked upwards and said, 'Father, I thank you for having heard me. I knew that you always hear me, but I have said this for the sake of the crowd standing here, so that they may believe that you sent me.' When he had said this, he cried with a loud voice, 'Lazarus, come out!' The dead man came out, his hands and feet bound with strips of cloth, and his face wrapped in a cloth. Jesus said to them, 'Unbind him, and let him go.'

Jesus is on his way to Jerusalem for the last time. He knows already, although his disciples don't, that a cruel and horrible death awaits him there. What sustains him is his extraordinary faith, his belief that because he is the bearer of God's purposes for Israel and the world, God will finally vindicate him by raising him from the dead. This faith draws on one of the great themes in some of the later prophetic books in the Old Testament, which declared that God's purpose for Israel was larger than they had yet seen. He was not content for them simply to go on being his people and forever struggling to lead righteous lives. When, at the end of all things, God made new heavens and new earth, he would raise all his people from death to share the new world. Just as when Ezekiel 37 speaks of Israel being raised from her grave, and Daniel 12 speaks of the righteous dead being raised to life, so Jesus understands his own mission as incorporating this extraordinary picture of new life, a life which can only come about by a mighty act of God.

As he travels on the Jerusalem road, he hears that one of his closest friends, Lazarus, the brother of Mary and Martha in Bethany, is sick. Then the news comes that he has died. To the surprise of the disciples, and the dismay of Mary and Martha, Jesus doesn't rush to heal the dying Lazarus and save his life. Rather, it appears that Jesus stays where he is and prays to God, asking that Lazarus be preserved from corruption, even though he has died, so that he can be restored to new life. When Jesus arrives in Bethany, he discovers that Lazarus is already dead and has been in the tomb for three full days. That is, of course, the time when corruption and decay would normally set in.

Martha, one of his close friends in that part of the country, meets him in deep distress and rebukes him: 'If you had been here, my brother would not have died.' But she goes on in verse 22, '...I know that God will give you whatever you ask of him.' It is as though she is reaching out, groping desperately for the possibility that Jesus might do something, even though such an act—the raising of the dead—is almost unheard of. Jesus tells her (v. 23) that her brother will rise again, but she assumes (v. 24) that he is simply referring to the resurrection on the last day. Most Jews of that period believed in such a resurrection, the time when God would create a new world and raise his people to new life.

At this point Jesus makes the boldest of statements: 'God's promises are coming true now, in me. I am the resurrection and the life. Those who believe in me, even though they die, will live, and everyone who lives and believes in me will never die.' And he challenges her, 'Do you believe this?' Martha, quite possibly saying more than she knows, replies, 'Yes, Lord, I believe that you are the Messiah, the Son of God, the one that God would send into the world.' Martha has grasped the central point that Jesus is the true king of Israel, the one through whom the promises of God would be fulfilled. What she may not yet have grasped is the fact that if Jesus is indeed this Messiah, he can, if he so wills, summon her brother Lazarus back from the grave.

Then Jesus approaches the tomb and meets Mary, the other sister who is also his close friend. Jesus is deeply disturbed and begins weeping (v. 35), but when he comes to the tomb (v. 38), he commands them to roll away the stone. Martha, always the practical one (as we know from elsewhere in the gospels), reminds him that Lazarus has been dead four days. If they removed the stone they would smell the stink of corrupting flesh. Jesus reassures her, reminding her that if she believed, she would see the glory of God. She would witness God the life-giver at work, raising the dead from the grave.

So the stone is removed; and the first words Jesus says are, 'Father, I thank you for having heard me.' I think this can only mean that, when the tomb was opened, there was no smell of corruption, and Jesus knew at once that God had acted. All he says next is, 'Lazarus, come out.' And the dead man comes out. The whole crowd witnesses the glory of God, God expressing the essence of his own self as creator, life-giver. It begins to prepare them for the even greater miracle which would occur a week or so later when Jesus was laid in a tomb and did more than return to his present life. He passed through death and emerged on the other side into utterly new life, the first fruit of God's new creation.

Give us, Father, the faith of Martha, that in recognizing Jesus as the true Messiah we may find in him the source of unending new life. Amen.

WEEK 5 (FRIDAY)

JOHN 12:20–26

Now among those who went up to worship at the festival were some Greeks. They came to Philip, who was from Bethsaida in Galilee, and said to him, 'Sir, we wish to see Jesus.' Philip went and told Andrew; then Andrew and Philip went and told Jesus. Jesus answered them, 'The hour has come for the Son of Man to be glorified. Very truly, I tell you, unless a grain of wheat falls into the earth and dies, it remains just a single grain; but if it dies, it bears much fruit. Those who love their life lose it, and those who hate their life in this world will keep it for eternal life. Whoever serves me must follow me, and where I am, there will my servant be also. Whoever serves me, the Father will honour.'

Jesus has arrived in Jerusalem for the Feast of the Passover. At the end of this last great journey, he is welcomed by crowds singing his praises and acclaiming him as Messiah. People have come from all over the known world for the feast; not only Jews but also some Greeks, quite possibly 'God-fearers', non-Jews who wanted to worship Israel's God but who had not taken the step of becoming actual proselytes. They come first to Philip, and tell him they want to see Jesus. Philip tells Andrew, and together they go and tell Jesus. And just when we expect Jesus to turn and address these Greeks, something quite different happens. Jesus sees that people from the wider world are coming to find him and wanting to speak to him, wanting to listen to him—and he receives this as part of the sign that the time has come for him to be glorified. He declares (v. 23), 'The hour has come for the Son of Man to be glorified.'

Throughout the New Testament, including in this Gospel, the glorifying of the Son of Man is connected with the vindication of Israel over the nations. A time will come when God's purpose will be fulfilled for Israel and through Israel for the world. How can this come about? Jesus seizes upon an image similar to one that he used many times in his parables, the image of the sower scattering seed. The seed sleeps in the earth and then rises, but the people who have sown it do not understand exactly why. They simply work and wait for the time of harvest. Now Jesus turns this image in a new direction.

In verse 24, he tells his listeners that unless a grain of wheat falls into the ground and dies, it remains alone, just a single grain; but when it dies it bears much fruit. What is he talking about? I think he is talking at two levels: about himself, but also about Israel. Israel has longed to hug to herself the purposes of God, affirming that she and she alone should be the people of God. Jesus has seen other so-called messiahs, other would-be leaders of Israel, encouraging Israel to think in that way, that she is the sole focus of God's concern. No, he says, the grain of wheat must fall into the earth and die, because only then can it bear much fruit. The city of Jerusalem is filled with Greeks, Romans, Syrians, Africans, Arabians—and they must all share in God's harvest. And not only them, but people across God's world are also waiting.

Jesus is not just talking at that level, of course; he is also talking about himself. He is Israel in person, he is the one who, like the grain of wheat, will fall into the earth and die. Otherwise he would simply be filling the air with useless words about himself and his few hearers. Through his death, however, he will bear much fruit. In verses 25 and 26, then, he issues a challenge to all those who follow him, both in his own day and subsequently. Those who love their life lose it; those who hate their life in this world will attain eternal life. And this 'eternal life' is to be understood in the Jewish sense of the age to come, not some timeless eternity but the dawning of a new day.

In our culture today there is a great deal that is turned in on itself, focusing on the world inside our heads, whether through virtual reality machines, portable stereos, or whatever. People create a little world around themselves and then go about bumping into other people, literally or metaphorically.

As Christians we are called to a very different attitude. We are called to be those whose lives reflect Jesus' life in being given to others, in being poured out for the world. I am not talking about hating life in a kind of self-destructive sense—though there are some Christians who have mistakenly thought that is what Jesus meant—but about the need to look at our lives in terms of the vocation to serve. We are called to give ourselves gladly to our fellow men and women, to the world, to be the people who will find this way of living reaffirmed in the new world that God makes.

And this is not something we can do apart from Jesus and from God (v. 26): 'Whoever serves me must follow me, and where I am, there will my servant be also.' This is the challenge that Jesus issued to Peter after the resurrection, when they met on the shore of the Sea of Galilee. Jesus said: Peter, follow me. I have trodden this way already. You must come after me and do what I have done, as my faithful servant. And where I am, there will you be also. Verse 26 indicates that this calling is for us all. 'Whoever serves me,' says Jesus, 'the Father will honour.' God is glorified by being truly himself, namely the life-giver, the lover, the healer (as we saw in John 11), and so Jesus is glorified when he works as the means by which God gives new life.

When we follow Jesus as his servants, we become people in whom the love of God is shed abroad in the world, and so we too are glorified. These words of Jesus come to us as words of vocation, which will mean different things to every person who hears them. Unless a grain of wheat falls into the earth and dies, it remains a single grain, and ultimately it will be lonely and old and have nothing to show for its life. But if it dies, it bears much fruit.

Sow in our hearts, gracious Lord, the seed of your own life and love, that we in turn may give our lives as seed that will bear fruit in your kingdom. Amen.

WEEK 5 (SATURDAY)

JOHN 12:27–36

'Now my soul is troubled. And what should I say—"Father, save me from this hour"? No, it is for this reason that I have come to this hour. Father, glorify your name.' Then a voice came from heaven, 'I have glorified it, and I will glorify it again.' The crowd standing there heard it and said that it was thunder. Others said, 'An angel has spoken to him.' Jesus answered, 'This voice has come for your sake, not for mine. Now is the judgement of this world; now the ruler of this world will be driven out. And I, when I am lifted up from the earth, will draw all people to myself.' He said this to indicate the kind of death he was to die. The crowd answered him, 'We have heard from the law that the Messiah remains for ever. How can you say that the Son of Man must be lifted up? Who is this Son of Man?' Jesus said to them, 'The light is with you for a little longer. Walk while you have the light, so that the darkness may not overtake you. If you walk in the darkness, you do not know where you are going. While you have the light, believe in the light, so that you may become children of light.' After Jesus had said this, he departed and hid from them.

Jesus has just announced a vocation for Israel, for his followers, but first and foremost for himself. And as he walks into the black depths of that vocation we should not be surprised that he says, 'Now my soul is troubled.' (v. 27) We see here an anticipation of the events in the Garden of Gethsemane, described in the other Gospels. Jesus reasons with himself: how can I possibly put my life totally at God's disposal? How can I go the way of the cross? What should I say—'Father, save me from this hour?' No, he says, it is precisely for this reason that I have come to this hour.

Whenever we are following in the way of the cross, a moment will come when we say, 'If only there were some other way. If only God would stop the world, would make something happen so I didn't have to go through this process.' Jesus prays in Gethsemane that the cup might pass from him, yet he still affirms God's will rather than his own. He has come to the climax of all he has been doing up to this point. And so he prays (v. 28), 'Father, glorify your name.' In other words: God my Father, be God my Father and be in and through me, so that the world may know and believe that you are God my Father.

Then a voice came from heaven. This happens very rarely in the Gospels. A voice spoke and said to him, 'I have glorified (my name), and I will glorify it again.' In other words, Jesus, as God's beloved Son, has brought glory to him. What Jesus is now going to do will bring even greater glory to God's name. God will be revealed in his full glory through this final work of Jesus.

As usual in John's Gospel, the crowd misunderstands what has happened. Some say that it was a thunderclap, some say that an angel has spoken to Jesus. And Jesus tells them that the voice has come for their sake, not for his. They need to know the significance of what is about to happen.

What they will see is a young would-be messiah led to his death at the hands of the pagans, a common enough sight in the first century. They have to realize, however, that this is the moment when Israel's destiny will be fulfilled, when God will pronounce judgment on the pagan world that is in rebellion against him, when he will vindicate his true people. This will be the moment when the forces of evil range themselves against God, but discover to their astonishment that even when they are doing what they characteristically do—killing people who get in their way—by that very means God will win the victory over them.

In verse 32, Jesus concludes his long answer to the question of verses 20 and 21, the question of the Greeks who have come to the feast and who want to see Jesus. He talks about being lifted up, being glorified, which John's readers know by now means being lifted up on the cross in the sight of all people. When Jesus is thus lifted up, Jews, Greeks, Romans, slaves—in fact everybody—will be drawn to the love of God. In other words, they will be drawn away from their allegiance to the rulers of this world who think they have it all in their grip, who think that by killing Jesus they are merely increasing their hold on God's creation. No, says Jesus, when they do that, they will ironically become the means by which the love of God is revealed. I will be lifted up and I will draw all people to myself.

Again the crowd admit that they don't understand. If he is the Messiah, he should reign in this world for ever. The Messiah ought to go on from glory to glory, leading his people in a victorious military revolution against the Romans. How can the Son of Man be lifted up? Who is this Son of Man? This is a question that New Testament scholars have argued about for many years, because Jesus does not provide a direct answer. He speaks about the light and the darkness. The light is with you a little longer, he says. Walk while you have the light, so that the darkness won't overtake you. If you walk in the darkness, turning away from me, from my embodiment of the saving, loving purposes of your one true God, then you will find yourself in outer darkness indeed. So while you have the chance, while you have the light, believe in it, so that you may become children of light.

In other words, while you have the true Israel, the Messiah, with you, believe in him so that you yourselves may be true Israel, God's people for the world. While you have among you the one who is shining God's light, believe in him so that you may in turn become the people of God through whom God will glorify his name. This vocation comes back to us again and again this Lent, and not only in Lent but every day in every generation. We must believe in the light of the love of God in Jesus, so that we, in turn, may become children of light. Then, through us, God can complete his purpose to draw all people to Jesus.

Grant, loving Lord, that we may walk in the light while we have it, and may reflect it to those around. Amen.

WEEK 6 (PASSION SUNDAY)

JOHN 13:1–20

Now before the festival of the Passover, Jesus knew that his hour had come to depart from this world and go to the Father. Having loved his own who were in the world, he loved them to the end. The devil had already put it into the heart of Judas son of Simon Iscariot to betray him. And during supper Jesus, knowing that the Father had given all things into his hands, and that he had come from God and was going to God, got up from the table, took off his outer robe, and tied a towel around himself. Then he poured water into a basin and began to wash the disciples' feet and to wipe them with the towel that was tied around him. He came to Simon Peter, who said to him, 'Lord, are you going to wash my feet?' Jesus answered, 'You do not know now what I am doing, but later you will understand.' Peter said to him, 'You will never wash my feet.' Jesus answered, 'Unless I wash you, you have no share with me.' Simon Peter said to him, 'Lord, not my feet only but also my hands and my head!' Jesus said to him, 'One who has bathed does not need to wash, except for the feet, but is entirely clean. And you are clean, though not all of you.' For he knew who was to betray him; for this reason he said, 'Not all of you are clean.'

After he had washed their feet, had put on his robe, and had returned to the table, he said to them, 'Do you know what I have done to you? You call me Teacher and Lord—and you are right, for that is what I am. So if I, your Lord and Teacher, have washed your feet, you also ought to wash one another's feet. For I have set you an example, that you also should do as I have done to you. Very truly, I tell you, servants are not greater than their master, nor are messengers greater than the one who sent them. If you know these things, you are blessed if you do them. I am not speaking of all of you; I know whom I have chosen. But it is to fulfil the scripture, "The one who ate my bread has lifted his heel against me." I tell you this now, before it occurs, so that when it does occur, you may believe that I am he. Very truly, I tell you, whoever receives one whom I send receives me; and whoever receives me receives him who sent me.'

We are now at the threshold of one of the greatest passages in the New Testament. In John 13–17 Jesus is with his disciples in the upper room on the night of his betrayal, arrest and trial; the night before his death. At this point in his narrative John gathers together the crux of Jesus' teaching, distilled through the apostle's own meditations on the Lord and his glory.

Interestingly, John does not describe the last supper itself in any detail. He merely says that Jesus arose from the meal table, so we can assume that the meal has already taken place. Back in the sixth chapter of John's Gospel Jesus speaks about eating his body and drinking his blood; here John focuses our attention in quite a different direction. It is really all contained in the very first verse: 'Before the festival of the Passover, Jesus knew that his hour had come to depart from this world and go to the Father. Having loved his own who were in the world, he loved them to the end.' For John—as in fact for most other New Testament writers—the Passover festival is the key to understanding what Jesus was going to accomplish. His death and resurrection would constitute the great act of exodus and liberation, setting God's people free just as the Passover celebrated the time when God led his people, under the shed blood of the lamb, through the Red Sea and off towards the promised land.

When John tells us (v. 1) that Jesus knew his hour had come, he is picking up a theme developed throughout the Gospel: Jesus' 'hour' was the moment when he was going to accomplish the mission for which he had been sent into the world. John characterizes this moment in terms of departing from the world and going to the Father, which is why the following chapters are known as the 'farewell discourses', when Jesus says goodbye to his followers. Still in the first verse of the passage, John says that Jesus had loved his followers 'to the end'. This phrase 'to the end' doesn't just mean that he went on loving them as long as there was breath in his body, although that was true as well. John clearly means that he loved them to the uttermost; there was nothing that love could do for them that he did not do for them. And this introduces us to the next scene, when Jesus enacts, symbolically, the love of God.

John notes that Judas, the son of Simon Iscariot, had already found it in his heart to betray Jesus. As betrayal involved an act of accusation, of accusing Jesus before the chief priests and the Jewish rulers, John attributes this betrayal to the devil, who in Hebrew has the name 'the Satan', which means 'the accuser'. Judas now personified the sense of accusation that had been hanging over Jesus for much of his ministry, and that was about to confront him openly. Verse 3, however, describes Jesus as knowing that the Father had given all things into his hands; he had come from God and was returning to God. His vocation until the very end of his earthly life was to be and do for Israel and the world what only God could be and do for them. He was committed to a course of action which was the very embodiment, or, to use the Latin word, the incarnation of the love of God.

After supper, to express that graphically, he got up from the table, took off his outer robe, tied a towel around himself, poured water into a basin and washed the disciples' feet. When John describes that sequence, he is describing not only the action of Jesus at the table but also the action of Jesus in coming down from God, laying aside the garments of his glory, taking instead the form of a servant, girding himself with a towel and doing for his friends the work that a servant would normally do. Washing the feet was a normal routine in most well-to-do houses, where it was the task of a slave to wash away the dust and dirt of the road from the feet of guests. Although this was a regular social courtesy, it was not one that would normally be performed by a social superior, let alone someone who was called Lord and Master.

There follows a little scene of what might almost be called comedy. Peter misunderstands. He does not want Jesus washing his feet. But Jesus insists: You don't understand this at the moment, he says to Peter, but you will later. Peter goes on blustering: I'm not going to let you wash my feet. And then Jesus responds, rather sharply: If I don't wash you, you can have no part in me, no share in what I'm doing. You must let me wash you. Peter's innate human pride means he doesn't want a humble leader. He might have to be humble in turn, and that would never do. But when he is faced with the threat that, unless he goes through with it, he won't have any part in Jesus' work, then, typically, he flips to the other extreme and says: You had better wash all of me—'Lord, not my feet only but also my hands and my head!' Jesus replies (v. 10), 'One who has bathed does not need to wash, except for the feet, but is entirely clean. And you are clean, though not all of you.' In other words, he has already accepted Peter; he has already cleansed him. But, as Peter walks on through the world, his feet will get dirty again and once more need washing. In the same way, when we pray the Lord's Prayer we don't have to start every time as totally unforgiven sinners. We come as God's beloved children, saying 'Our Father in heaven', but halfway through the prayer we admit gladly and freely that we have some things that need sorting out, some problems that need addressing today. And it will be the same tomorrow.

So Jesus washes his disciples' feet, and explains to Peter what it means, how it connects with their sharing in his life, his glory, his work. When he has finished, put on his robe again, and returned to the table, he explains further to them the significance of what he has done. This combination of acted symbol, followed by explanation, was typical of the Old Testament prophet. Well, he says, you call me Teacher and Lord (v. 13), and you are right to do so, because that is what I am. You must learn, though, that if your Lord and Teacher has washed your feet, you also should wash one another's feet. Jesus is deliberately standing the normal social order on its head, turning the values of the world upside-down. He reminds them that servants are not greater than their master (v. 16) nor messengers than the one who sent them. In other words, because they are his servants, his messengers, they can and must follow his example and nothing else.

Throughout all this, Jesus is aware that one of those sitting at the table, one of those whose feet he has washed, is about to get up and leave the company, never to return. The only time they will see him again is when he appears in the garden to betray his master. Jesus is less concerned about that, however, than about conveying to the disciples the meaning of his action. This is what it means to be equal with God, to reveal the glory of God. Loving his followers to the uttermost, he wants to bequeath them this new way of life which is no less than embodying the love of God—love that was expressed uniquely in Jesus, but then given by his Spirit to all his followers.

Jesus, master and Lord, teach us by your loving service how to serve one another in love, that we may in turn embody the love of the Father. Amen.

WEEK 6 (MONDAY)

JOHN 13:21–38

After saying this Jesus was troubled in spirit, and declared, 'Very truly, I tell you, one of you will betray me.' The disciples looked at one another, uncertain of whom he was speaking. One of his disciples—the one whom Jesus loved—was reclining next to him; Simon Peter therefore motioned to him to ask Jesus of whom he was speaking. So while reclining next to Jesus, he asked him, 'Lord, who is it?' Jesus answered, 'It is the one to whom I give this piece of bread when I have dipped it in the dish.' So when he had dipped the piece of bread, he gave it to Judas son of Simon Iscariot. After he received the piece of bread, Satan entered into him. Jesus said to him, 'Do quickly what you are going to do.' Now no one at the table knew why he said this to him. Some thought that, because Judas had the common purse, Jesus was telling him, 'Buy what we need for the festival'; or, that he should give something to the poor. So, after receiving the piece of bread, he immediately went out. And it was night.

When he had gone out, Jesus said, 'Now the Son of Man has been glorified, and God has been glorified in him. If God has been glorified in him, God will also glorify him in himself and will glorify him at once. Little children, I am with you only a little longer. You will look for me; and as I said to the Jews so now I say to you, "Where I am going, you cannot come." I give you a new commandment, that you love one another. Just as I have loved you, you also should love one another. By this everyone will know that you are my disciples, if you have love for one another.'

Simon Peter said to him, 'Lord, where are you going?' Jesus answered, 'Where I am going, you cannot follow me now; but you will follow afterwards.' Peter said to him, 'Lord, why can I not follow you now? I will lay down my life for you.' Jesus answered, 'Will you lay down your life for me? Very truly, I tell you, before the cock crows, you will have denied me three times.'

The story now moves first to Judas' act of betrayal and then to Jesus' prediction of Peter's denial. Within the narrative movement of these chapters we find in miniature the narrative movement of the Gospel as a whole: Jesus came to his own and his own didn't receive him. Here he is loving his own, his own twelve friends; one of them will betray him, and another will deny him. In verse 21 we read that Jesus was 'troubled in spirit'; his reading of the scriptural passages, his observation of Judas, and his deep knowledge of each one of his followers, told him that all was not well. Someone present at this most intimate of moments was about to betray him to the chief priests.

It's an interesting reflection on the other disciples that they could not guess whom he was talking about. When we see paintings of the last supper, or read lists of the disciples, we see things from after the event: Judas Iscariot always comes at the end of the lists, with a note that he was the one who would be the traitor, and in the paintings he is marked out as different. It is clear from this passage, though, that the other eleven didn't look around the table, murmuring, 'Aha, we know who that will be, it must be old Judas over there.' In fact they were genuinely troubled and uncertain. The disciple whom Jesus loved (by long tradition seen as John, although that is always a matter of debate) asked Jesus who it was. By way of answer, Jesus used a sign of special friendship and affection traditional at meal-times, when the host would dip a piece of bread in a sauce and give it to somebody whom he wished to favour. Jesus did this, and gave it to Judas, the son of Simon Iscariot. 'After he received the piece of bread,' says John, 'Satan entered into him'; this I think means that he became 'the accuser' from that moment on. He became the one who would point the finger at Jesus, saying, 'This is the man you must arrest.'

Jesus said to him (v. 27), 'Do quickly what you are going to do.' Nobody at the table understood why he said that. They did not assume that this identified Judas as a traitor. They simply thought he had some small task to attend to. But, says John, immediately after receiving the piece of bread, Judas went out. 'And it was night.' That last sentence is one of the most famous lines in John's Gospel, just three little words in the Greek text. Not only was there a brief glimpse into the darkness, as some of the disciples looked up and saw Judas disappear into the night; Judas was leaving the company of those called to be the light of the world, and choosing to go into the darkness where he would make common cause with the accuser, the Satan.

After the door shuts behind Judas (v. 31 onwards), a sense of excitement builds as those who are left now hear the deepest truth. Now that Judas has gone, something very precious, very secret, can be revealed. This secret is fundamentally concerned with glory and love. Jesus begins by saying (v. 31): 'Now the Son of Man has been glorified.' The accuser is on his way; and when he accuses the Son of Man, the Son of Man will be lifted up, vindicated, exalted. This will fulfil the purpose of God. God will glorify Jesus, and glorify him at once.

This, he is explaining, is the purpose for which he was born; this is why he came as Israel's representative, the Son of Man. This is what he was made for; this, so to speak, is what God was made for. This is God's way of expressing his own self most fully. And it was going to happen there and then. Jesus then tells them (v. 33) that he can only be with them a little longer. Then he must go and do a task with which they cannot help. Peter is about to get angry: he's always accompanied Jesus up to now, and he doesn't see why he should stop doing so. But Jesus is quite clear that nobody can follow him in what he is going to do. Instead (vv. 34 and 35), he bequeaths to them his way of life, his way of glory, which is the way of love. 'I give you a new commandment.' We can imagine him saying it with almost breathless excitement. 'This is how you will be characterized as the true Israel, the people in whom the living God will be at work. You must love one another as I have loved you.' They must remember the washing of the feet, and realize that that is how they must love one another.

And in verse 35, Jesus tells them that in this way everybody will know them as his disciples. Reading the passage two thousand years later, we can both agree and lament the fact that it has not exactly happened like that. Would that Jesus' people loved one another as he loved them; whenever this love appears, a new way of living comes into being, one which still puts to shame the rest of the world with its cynical politics, manoeuvrings and back-stabbings. Within the church we should live in a way which declares that we are the disciples of Jesus, the ones in whom God is glorified.

At this point, once again, Peter is a source of irony. He insists that he will follow Jesus, adding in verse 37 that he will even lay down his life for him. In answer, Jesus speaks one of the most ironic lines in the whole Gospel: 'Will you lay down your life for me?' Peter has not yet understood that the Good Shepherd must give his life for the sheep. The Son of Man must be lifted up, exalted on the cross, to draw all people to himself. Can Peter really lay down his life to save Jesus? Of course not. Jesus is on his way to lay down his life to save Peter, completing on the cross the great work to which the washing of the feet pointed. Peter had not wanted him to do that, either. In both cases, Jesus has to say: Sorry, Peter, this is the way it must be. And, what is more, 'before the cock crows, you will have denied me three times.' That was the last thing Peter wanted to hear. It was the last thing that he thought would actually happen. But, as we know, that was the path he took, while Jesus went unaccompanied to his death, to reveal the glory of the Father's love.

Give us, Father, such a measure of your love, that we may love one another and so reveal your glory. Amen.

WEEK 6 (TUESDAY)

JOHN 14:1–7

'Do not let your hearts be troubled. Believe in God, believe also in me. In my Father's house there are many dwelling-places. If it were not so, would I have told you that I go to prepare a place for you? And if I go and prepare a place for you, I will come again and will take you to myself, so that where I am, there you may be also. And you know the way to the place where I am going.' Thomas said to him, 'Lord, we do not know where you are going. How can we know the way?' Jesus said to him, 'I am the way, and the truth, and the life. No one comes to the Father except through me. If you know me, you will know my Father also. From now on you do know him and have seen him.'

From this point on, Jesus knows that he is going away from the disciples. He is going tonight, going this Passion-tide, going to the cross, to a place of utter loneliness where all will forsake him. But he is also going away in the sense that they will no longer have him with them day by day, week by week, walking through Palestine as before. He must therefore open to them the secrets of how they are going to follow him, how they will be his people for the world, what will happen after he has gone.

He begins by telling them not to let their hearts be troubled, disturbed, or stirred up. 'Do not fear' is the single most repeated command throughout the Bible. Jesus was echoing what one Old Testament writer after another had said. And the reason why their hearts should not be troubled is because they believe in God. Throughout their time with Jesus they have been clinging to their belief in God. Now they must trust him, when he tells them that in his Father's house there are many dwelling places—for how else could he go and prepare a place for them?

This is a difficult passage, and various translations have been offered. It seems to be describing the purpose of God to create a whole new world, one in which there would be plenty of room, and a warm welcome, for every one of God's children. Even if they have to follow Jesus to suffering and death, they will not miss the way. Rather, the very suffering will become the way leading to their particular dwelling-place in the house of God. Jesus reassures them that he is going to prepare the place for them, before returning and taking them to himself, so that they will be wherever he is.

This seems to contain two promises: one referring to the end of their lives, when Jesus will come and take them to himself after they die, and another, to be fulfilled more immediately. This will take place after Jesus has passed through death and into the world of the resurrection age, when he will return in his risen body to assure them that they are now his people, part of the new world that God has already begun. Teasingly (v. 4) he says to them, 'You know the way to the place where I am going.' Hardly surprisingly, Thomas (who, as one commentator says, always appears as a loyal but dull disciple) expresses what, no doubt, they are all feeling. 'No, Lord,' he says. 'We do not know where you are going. How can we know the way?' And Jesus answers (v. 6), 'I am the way, and the truth, and the life.' Or, as some people have suggested, the Greek may better be translated, 'I am the true and living way.' No one comes to the Father except through Jesus. Whoever knows Jesus knows his Father also.

What is Jesus saying in this climactic verse? He is re-emphasizing his task and vocation both as the human being, Jesus of Nazareth, and as Israel's representative Messiah. As we saw in the prologue at the beginning of this Gospel, Jesus came as the word of God, to dwell, to tabernacle, in our midst. He is the fulfilment of those strange prophetic passages in the Old Testament that spoke of the one true and living God coming to live with his people. Some scholars and writers argue that no first-century Jew could ever think of a human being as God incarnate, and that therefore a passage like this must reflect a much later perspective. This ignores, however, the fact that first-century Jews did believe in the word of God speaking within Israel, the breath of God breathing into the life of the world, and the presence of God above all in the temple in Jerusalem.

Jesus has drawn precisely these themes on to himself. If he is Israel's Messiah, then he is the one who is completing God's purpose; but no one can complete God's purpose except God himself. It is thus within the intimate relationship Jesus describes between himself and his Father that we see the key to the problem with which theologians for hundreds of years would wrestle. It is the problem of how a human being, Jesus of Nazareth, could be the window through whom we see the true nature of God, the one in whom the living presence of God resides. Verse 7 encapsulates the idea: from that point on, all who have seen and known Jesus know and see the Father also. It is a challenge to each of us, particularly in Lent, to realize that in looking at Jesus we discover the creator of the universe, and in discovering him, we know him as our Father, just as Jesus did.

Lord Jesus Christ, lead us in the way which is your own self; that we may hold firm to your truth, and share your undying life. Amen.

WEEK 6 (WEDNESDAY)

JOHN 14:8–14

Philip said to him, 'Lord, show us the Father, and we will be satisfied.' Jesus said to him, 'Have I been with you all this time, Philip, and you still do not know me? Whoever has seen me has seen the Father. How can you say, "Show us the Father"? Do you not believe that I am in the Father and the Father is in me? The words that I say to you I do not speak on my own; but the Father who dwells in me does his works. Believe me that I am in the Father and the Father is in me; but if you do not, then believe me because of the works themselves. Very truly, I tell you, the one who believes in me will also do the works that I do and, in fact, will do greater works than these, because I am going to the Father. I will do whatever you ask in my name, so that the Father may be glorified in the Son. If in my name you ask me for anything, I will do it.'

Thomas has had his turn at asking what seems like the idiot's question. Now it is Philip's turn. Jesus has stated that everybody who has been with him knows the Father through him. Philip's response is: Show us the Father, then, and that'll be enough for us. Then Jesus makes another remarkable claim (v. 9): 'Have I been with you all this time, Philip, and you still do not know me? Whoever has seen me has seen the Father.' Jesus is the transparent window on the inner life of God. What Jesus has done, climaxing already in the foot-washing but now going on to his death on the cross, reveals the very heart of God. We can thus know God in a way more intimate than any philosophy, abstract idea, symbol, or icon. This is what it means to be equal with God. We understand God as we see him take human form and come to pour himself out in the final actualization of his eternally giving love.

Philip, therefore, has got it wrong. What he needs to see (v. 10) is that Jesus is in the Father and the Father is in him. All that Jesus is doing is surrounded by the fatherhood of God, the glory of God. When he speaks to them, he is not speaking on his own authority. He is doing the work, speaking the words, of the Father who is dwelling in him. Jesus speaks, again almost teasingly, to Philip (v. 11): 'Believe me that I am in the Father and the Father is in me.' If they find it difficult to believe, they should think back to all that he has done. They need to remember the wedding at Cana, the healing of the centurion's servant, the coming to faith of the woman of Samaria, the wilderness feeding, the healing of the man born blind. They must remember, supremely, the raising of Lazarus from the dead. Lastly, mysteriously, they must remember the washing of the disciples' feet. This is the evidence that John shows to his readers, evidence that Jesus was indeed in the Father and the Father was indeed in him.

Then he says something surprising, and indeed challenging, to all his followers (v. 12): 'The one who believes in me will also do the works that I do and, in fact, will do greater works than these, because I am going to the Father.' I have difficulty knowing precisely what Jesus meant by this. How could his followers do greater works than him? I am sure, though, that he did not mean that his followers would do lesser works than him, which is how we tend to understand it. We argue that Jesus did remarkable deeds because he was God incarnate, because the Spirit was with him. We, however, think of ourselves as poor creatures, feeble even in our prayer: how could we think of attempting anything for God? Nevertheless, this promise remains literally and metaphorically on the books; and it is accompanied by the command to pray. In verse 13, Jesus says he will do whatever they ask in his name, so that the Father may be glorified in the Son. And he repeats this promise in the next verse: 'If in my name you ask me for anything, I will do it.'

Of course this is not just a general invitation. It is not a matter of a Christian grabbing a whim that comes into mind, sending up a casual prayer and having it granted. As is often pointed out, the key phrase is 'in my name'. In the ancient Middle East, somebody's name was the clue to their character. When Jesus talks about asking 'in my name' he means 'in my character'. If his followers live the life that he is living, then they can only ask for something that is an appropriate expression of that life, something that will bring glory to God through Jesus the Son. And of course God will give it to them. We are often genuinely unsure whether or not a particular request will be for God's glory in the present time. I suspect, however, that we tend to err on the side of over-caution, deciding that we had better not ask in case we look foolish or are proved wrong. But if Jesus truly is as John has presented him, if the Father truly is who Jesus made him out to be, then surely we should err on the other side. We should be saying, 'To the best of our knowledge, this is what we should be praying for; therefore we shall ask for it in the name of the Son, so that the Father may be glorified.'

God longs to express himself fully through Jesus and through Jesus' people. Jesus wants to do fully all that he has been sent to do, working to the glory of God. He wants us to do and be all that we are intended to do and be. The only way we will accomplish that is through constant prayer. We must pray for the work of God in us and though us, pray for the glory of God to be seen in us and through us, pray for the love of God to shine in us and through us.

Reading this whole paragraph—verses 8 to 14—we arrive at a frightening conclusion. Jesus announces at the beginning of the paragraph that whoever has seen him has seen the Father, and he gives us the evidence of the work that the Father has been doing through him. At the end of the paragraph he says that those who follow him and believe in him will do all these works and greater works still, in answer to prayer, so that the Father may be glorified. Our conclusion must be that the church should be working in such a way that, when challenged, we could point to it as proof of what God is doing. Even writing that feels and sounds almost blasphemous, which only goes to show how far short we are from this ideal. Nevertheless, as we shall see, John goes on in the next part of these discourses to amplify these statements, showing how, through the work of the followers of Jesus, God can and will be glorified.

Help us, Lord Jesus, so to know you that when we pray in your name we may ask according to your will. Amen.

WEEK 6 (THURSDAY)

JOHN 14:15–31

'If you love me, you will keep my commandments. And I will ask the Father, and he will give you another Advocate, to be with you for ever. This is the Spirit of truth, whom the world cannot receive, because it neither sees him nor knows him. You know him, because he abides with you, and he will be in you.

'I will not leave you orphaned; I am coming to you. In a little while the world will no longer see me, but you will see me; because I live, you also will live. On that day you will know that I am in my Father, and you in me, and I in you. They who have my commandments and keep them are those who love me; and those who love me will be loved by my Father, and I will love them and reveal myself to them.' Judas (not Iscariot) said to him, 'Lord, how is it that you will reveal yourself to us, and not to the world?' Jesus answered him, 'Those who love me will keep my word, and my Father will love them, and we will come to them and make our home with them. Whoever does not love me does not keep my words; and the word that you hear is not mine, but is from the Father who sent me.

'I have said these things to you while I am still with you. But the Advocate, the Holy Spirit, whom the Father will send in my name, will teach you everything, and remind you of all that I have said to you. Peace I leave with you; my peace I give to you. I do not give to you as the world gives. Do not let your hearts be troubled, and do not let them be afraid. You heard me say to you, "I am going away, and I am coming to you." If you loved me, you would rejoice that I am going to the Father, because the Father is greater than I. And now I have told you this before it occurs, so that when it does occur, you may believe. I will no longer talk much with you, for the ruler of this world is coming. He has no power over me; but I do as the Father has commanded me, so that the world may know that I love the Father. Rise, let us be on our way.'

Throughout John's Gospel we have seen Jesus doing and saying things that only make sense if it is true that God gives to his followers the same Spirit who dwelt within Jesus and who would enable them to continue his work in the world. It is in this chapter, from verse 15 onwards, that this promise becomes explicit. As we saw a few days ago, Jesus said something similar in John 7; but that was no more than a passing comment, compared to the way it is spelt out here.

This promise of the Spirit's coming is framed by the command to love. If you love me, says Jesus, you will keep my commandments; you will follow in the way that I have led. And for those who believe, who are cleansed by the death of Jesus, and renewed by his resurrection life, he will ask the Father to give another advocate. The word 'advocate' has many different meanings, including 'comforter', and 'helper.' It is also a legal term: an advocate is one who stands up for somebody in a court of law. It can even refer to a very personal relationship, meaning one who comes alongside somebody in distress to comfort them and give them strength. All this is encompassed in the role of the Spirit of whom Jesus speaks—'the Spirit of truth', as he says in verse 17. The world beyond the present circle of Jesus' followers cannot receive the Spirit of truth, being unable to see him or know him. But the disciples know him because he abides with them already, and will remain within them. The Spirit, therefore, becomes Jesus' alter ego, Jesus' second self. Jesus himself will die, and after his resurrection will go to be with the Father. His followers will see him no more but they will feel no sense of absence. Instead they will sense his presence in a different way.

For the last two or three hundred years in the West we have lived in a very materialistic universe, and we find it very difficult to think of different levels of reality intermingling. This, however, is what John invites us to do here. The Spirit of Jesus, the Spirit of the living God who dwelt in Jesus, can so breathe into the life of ordinary men, women and children that, far from Jesus being distant or absent, he will be truly present. As he tells his followers in verse 18, 'I will not leave you orphaned.' He will not be like a father who disappears so that his children never see him again. In a little while, he will be gone from the world. The world will celebrate a triumph over him, and, even while he is appearing in his risen body to his disciples, the rest of the world will know nothing of it, and will refuse to believe it when they do hear of it. His followers will see him, though, risen in new life. On that day (v. 20) they will know that he is in the Father and, this time, they will know that they are in him. The intimate relationship between Father and Son is not a closed circle, for ever barred to outsiders. By the gift of the Spirit, others will be welcomed into that intimacy, that inner circle of the love of God.

And who are these others? Verse 21 explains that they are those who have Jesus' commandments and keep them. As they love him, so they will be loved by the Father and by Jesus himself. Here again we have a disciple with a walk-on part, declaring (as well he might) that he doesn't understand what's going on. This time it's the other Judas, not Judas Iscariot. He cannot understand how Jesus can make himself known to them but not to the world. All along they have been waiting for a great act of God which will show the whole world in a flash that Jesus is the true Messiah, that his followers were right to obey his call. Jesus does not answer Judas directly. He simply gives him and the others a commission: if they love him, they will keep his commands, and his Father will love them too. And Father and Son together will come and make their home with them.

Jesus must have been aware throughout his ministry, but particularly now as he is preparing for the end, how little his followers understood. So he explains that the task of the Holy Spirit is not simply to embody his presence with them, but to teach them all that they cannot understand, all that they would otherwise forget, all that they will need to know as they go out into the world in his name. He can, therefore, give them the supreme gift of peace, his peace (v. 27).

The world offers a certain style of peace. The Emperor Augustus offered the world *Pax Romana*, peace under Roman imperial rule. His successor Tiberius maintained that he too had kept the world reasonably peaceful; but it was always peace at a price, and it was always somebody else who paid that price in the Roman Empire. Peace was maintained through violence and force. Jesus creates peace and gives peace by giving his own life. And in verse 27 he repeats the command from verse 1: 'Do not let your hearts be troubled, and do not let them be afraid.' As far as he can, Jesus has prepared them for what will happen. When he is taken from them, it will still be a great shock and they will not understand it, but they will nevertheless reflect on what he told them beforehand. He therefore warns them (v. 30) that 'the ruler of this world' is coming: the one with earthly power, the one who speaks with authority from Rome. But even he has no absolute power over Jesus. He can wield only the power given him from above. Jesus submits to him only in order to fulfil what the Father has commanded, to demonstrate to the world that he loves the Father and is obedient to what he has been commanded. As a result of his faithfulness to his commission, God will be glorified. And as a further result of that faithfulness, the disciples will find, to their surprise, that they are enfolded within the very life of God himself, the inner life of God, Father, Son and Spirit. They will share in the glory that was Jesus' glory, as they too are commissioned to go and bear fruit.

Send to us your own Spirit, gracious Lord, that we may know your presence and your peace. Amen.

WEEK 6 (FRIDAY)

JOHN 15:1–11

'I am the true vine, and my Father is the vine-grower. He removes every branch in me that bears no fruit. Every branch that bears fruit he prunes to make it bear more fruit. You have already been cleansed by the word that I have spoken to you. Abide in me as I abide in you. Just as the branch cannot bear fruit by itself unless it abides in the vine, neither can you unless you abide in me. I am the vine, you are the branches. Those who abide in me and I in them bear much fruit, because apart from me you can do nothing. Whoever does not abide in me is thrown away like a branch and withers; such branches are gathered, thrown into the fire, and burned. If you abide in me, and my words abide in you, ask for whatever you wish, and it will be done for you. My Father is glorified by this, that you bear much fruit and become my disciples. As the Father has loved me, so I have loved you; abide in my love. If you keep my commandments, you will abide in my love, just as I have kept my Father's commandments and abide in his love. I have said these things to you so that my joy may be in you, and that your joy may be complete.'

Jesus now picks up yet one more important Jewish image. In Psalm 80 the psalmist had spoken of God bringing a vine out of Egypt, a vine that represented Israel. God drove out the nations and planted Israel as his own people in his own land. The psalmist goes on to tell how every passer-by was plucking its grapes, the wild boars were ravaging it and the beasts of the field devouring it. Isaiah, similarly, writes a poem about the vineyard of the Lord of hosts, the house of Israel (Isaiah 5). It is like a vine that has produced wild grapes, and which is therefore under God's judgment. With the resonance of these strange and sad images of the vine in mind, Jesus now declares himself the true vine. He is the true Israel, the true Messiah. It is far more than a familiar image drawn from the farms and fields of Palestine. Jesus is evoking a powerful Old Testament symbol for the whole vocation that he has embraced. He is the true vine, and his Father is, of course, the vine-grower, who removes all the branches that bear no fruit, and prunes every fertile branch to make it even more fruitful. While I have never pruned a vine, I do know that when you prune a rose bush, you encourage the bush to grow fewer, stronger flowers rather than a mass of tiny ones. The plant is actually made healthier by the pruning knife.

Such pruning implies bearing a certain amount of pain. Jesus knew his disciples would have to learn a great deal as they attempted to live for him in the world. They were beginning to bear fruit. Those who were not bearing fruit had already been removed (v. 2)— perhaps a reference to Judas. They are assured, however, that they have already been cleansed (v. 3); the same Greek word is used here to refer to both cleansing and pruning, as though the activity of pruning keeps the plant healthy by cleansing away dirt.

Then Jesus tells them in verse 4 that they must abide, dwell in him, as he promises to dwell in them. This is part of the continuing vine illustration. If you cut a branch off a vine, it may look fine for a while, maybe even a day or so if it is a large branch. Before long, though, the leaves wither and the branch dies, never to bear any more grapes. The branch can only be fruitful if it remains in the parent stem, drawing on its energy, life and fruitfulness. So Jesus says (v. 5): 'I am the vine, you are the branches. Those who abide in me and I in them bear much fruit, because apart from me you can do nothing.'

How easy it is for Christians, then or now, to imagine that as soon as they have received a few words from Jesus, they can charge off, do whatever comes into their head, and expect God to bless it. Instead, we must live faithfully within the life of Jesus and allow his life to be lived out through us. Those who detach themselves, like branches pulled away from the vine, are good for nothing except to be thrown into the fire and burned like worthless, dead wood. If we do abide in Jesus, the promise is repeated (v. 7) that whatever we ask for in prayer will be done for us. This is how God fulfils his purpose, becoming truly God of all the world in the way that he always wanted to be. It will happen through Jesus' people at work in the world, becoming his disciples, bearing fruit, glorifying the Father.

What then does it mean to abide in Jesus, in his love? We have seen in chapter 13 what the love of Jesus looks like when he gets up from the table and washes the disciples' feet. There is a way of love, a pattern of love, which is the Jesus pattern, and that is the pattern we must follow as his disciples. It is not something we do at a distance, copying Jesus with a vague memory of what he did. We live it out through prayer and sacrament, giving us day by day the energy to do and be for our world what Jesus was for his. Nor should we suppose that this calling lays a heavy burden on us, pulling us down into perpetual gloom. Far from it. If we keep his commandments we will abide in his love, never to be separated from it. If we carry out his commission we will know his presence and his love surrounding us.

We might expect at the end of such an awesome commission a warning of the dangers of falling short, of failing to reach the standard. Not a bit of it (v. 11): 'I have said these things to you so that my joy may be in you, and that your joy may be complete.' God is glorified through the work of Jesus and the obedience of his followers—but joy is given, as well as glory. The joy that Jesus has, the joy of knowing that he is in the centre of the Father's will and purpose, is given to all his followers too. This is what it means to follow Jesus. And it is just as well because, as we shall see in the passages that follow, the world will oppose us. We need to be assured of the joy of God welling up deep within us, so that, like Jesus, we can face the fight and fury of the enemy.

Enable us, Father, to abide in Jesus, that we may bear fruit that will last. Amen.

Week 6 (Saturday)

John 15:12–17

'This is my commandment, that you love one another as I have loved you. No one has greater love than this, to lay down one's life for one's friends. You are my friends if you do what I command you. I do not call you servants any longer, because the servant does not know what the master is doing; but I have called you friends, because I have made known to you everything that I have heard from my Father. You did not choose me but I chose you. And I appointed you to go and bear fruit, fruit that will last, so that the Father will give you whatever you ask him in my name. I am giving you these commands so that you may love one another.'

Jesus has revealed to his followers what love really looks like. He is going to complete that revelation on the cross. As a result, precisely because they are his followers, his disciples, he wants them to copy him to the uttermost, which means that they must love one another in the same way that he has loved them. They must show in their own life together that same quality of self-giving, self-effacing love that Jesus had shown and would show supremely on the cross.

In verse 13, he summarizes: 'No one has greater love than this, to lay down one's life for one's friends.' This text has been much misused by generations of preachers and orators urging young people (often young men) to go off and lay down their life in war. Although that may summon up a noble spirit of self-sacrifice, what Jesus is describing is something far greater than fighting a war, a conflict resulting from the failure to negotiate peace. Jesus is talking about the self-giving of an entire life, minute by minute, day by day, year by year. It is easy for us to be cynical about genuine love, to imagine that people are acting merely from a desire for status, for good reputation. What Jesus is describing goes deeper than any self-seeking, deeper than any self-serving. It simply wants to do the utmost possible for the beloved, up to and including the point of giving its own life.

And he tells his followers (vv. 14 and 15) that if they do that, they are his friends. He could have called them servants—in one sense he was the master and they the servants, and that is how they have regarded him all along. In the end, though, the servant does not understand what the master is doing. As we saw in the book of Revelation, the true worship of the people of God is not a knee-jerk reaction, but a considered response to the love of God and the greatness of God in creation and redemption. In the same sense, Jesus wants his followers to be his friends, who have sat round the table with him and understood his purposes. He is sharing with them the innermost secrets of his life, secrets so great and so awesome that they can be expressed only in acted symbols or in these stark simplicities. 'Love one another as I have loved you'—what could be so simple, yet so profound and, as we all know, so hard to put into practice?

Jesus calls his disciples 'friends' because he has made known to them everything that he has heard from the Father, sharing his heavenly commission with them. And he assures them that they did not choose him. Rather, he chose them. They were as surprised as anyone when he came along the shore by Capernaum or stopped by Matthew's tax-collecting booth and said, 'I want you to follow me.' Jesus chose them and appointed them to go and, like branches in a vine, to bear fruit, lasting fruit. And yet again comes the promise that the Father will give whatever they ask in his name. Jesus has used the picture of the vine to show how he and his followers are held together in the life of love, held together because he is the vine and they are the branches. He now commissions them to be people of love, people who will go out into the world to spread that love everywhere.

Lord Jesus, as you have called us your friends, help us so to understand what you are doing, that we may gladly do your work and reveal your glory. Amen.

JOHN 15:18–27

'If the world hates you, be aware that it hated me before it hated you. If you belonged to the world, the world would love you as its own. Because you do not belong to the world, but I have chosen you out of the world—therefore the world hates you. Remember the word that I said to you, "Servants are not greater than their master." If they persecuted me, they will persecute you; if they kept my word, they will keep yours also. But they will do all these things to you on account of my name, because they do not know him who sent me. If I had not come and spoken to them, they would not have sin; but now they have no excuse for their sin. Whoever hates me hates my Father also. If I had not done among them the works that no one else did, they would not have sin. But now they have seen and hated both me and my Father. It was to fulfil the word that is written in their law, "They hated me without a cause."

'When the Advocate comes, whom I will send to you from the Father, the Spirit of truth who comes from the Father, he will testify on my behalf. You also are to testify because you have been with me from the beginning.'

On Palm Sunday Jesus was, outwardly at least, a success—perhaps more than at any time in his life. People were waving palm branches and shouting, hailing him as a conquering hero as he rode into the city on a donkey. And yet, as we know from Luke's Gospel, he was riding in tears because he knew that the city was rejecting his way of peace. During the following week, the crowds that had shouted 'Hosanna' gradually fell away from him until his last night when only his disciples were left with him, and even they abandoned him at the end. What Jesus was offering was deep and rich, but strange—too much of a challenge to their way of life, denying all that they would have expected to gain from victory over their enemies. They could not take the message that he offered, and so he had to come to terms with rejection. He speaks of that rejection in our passage today: John 15:18–27.

Jesus came to his own, but they did not receive him. He was in the world, the world that he had made, but it did not recognize him. When he commissioned his disciples to be the branches of the vine that was his own life, his own work, he knew from the beginning that they would face the same opposition as he did. He was hated by the world because he was different, showing up the shallowness and triviality, the deficiency and destructiveness of so much that passed for human life. Jesus could see that if his followers, even for a moment, lived by his command to love one another, they would encounter the same thing, hatred (v. 18): 'If the world hates you, be aware that it hated me before it hated you.' If they had simply belonged to the world (v. 19), if they were simply offering a new religion—and the world was full of new religions—that would have been different. But Jesus has chosen them out of the world, and therefore the world will be deeply threatened. And when people are threatened, they hate.

The disciples were commissioned to challenge the whole structure of the world, the way people went about their business, the way they organized their personal and communal lives. They were to live differently, and that was bound to cause trouble. Jesus reminds them again (v. 20) that servants are not greater than their master. People persecuted Jesus, and will persecute his followers. Likewise, looking on the positive side for a moment, if they kept Jesus' word, they will keep the disciples' word also. And when the disciples are hated because of their allegiance to Jesus, they must cling on to one thing (v. 21): this is happening to them because of Jesus' name. This is the other aspect of the power of Jesus' name. When we pray in his name and according to his will, we can be sure that our prayer is heard and answered. Likewise, when we act in Jesus' name, then just as people opposed him, so they will oppose us.

Jesus puts in a mitigating clause (v. 22): if he had not come and spoken to them, they would not have sin. Now, however, they have less than no excuse for their opposition and they are condemned for rejecting God the Father when they reject his son (v. 23). Jesus has embodied the Father's will, so if somebody is hating him, that person is hating God as well. He repeats this message in verse 24:

if he had not done his unique works among them, they would not have sin. If Jesus had simply come to give good advice, people could have remained interested but mainly sceptical. But the works of Jesus recorded in John's Gospel, from turning water into wine to the raising of Lazarus, left people no choice. They could accept that he was who he said he was, or denounce him as in league with Beelzebub, working with the authority of some occult power.

All this has happened (v. 25) to fulfil a word that was written in the Psalms, which testify to the anxiety and struggle caused when people oppose the children of God. They hated Jesus without a cause. What had he done? Given the blind their sight, made the lame walk, raised the dead; and yet people turned on him. People had so much cause to love him, and yet, because he had shone the light of God into the world, those who preferred the darkness were bound to reject him as a threat.

Then Jesus sets out, as it were, a court case between his followers and those who will hate them without cause. How can his followers cope when they find themselves in court, literally or metaphorically? What they need is an advocate, and that is what Jesus promises them (v. 26): 'When the Advocate comes, whom I will send to you from the Father, the Spirit of truth who comes from the Father, he will testify on my behalf.' In other words, whenever we are in the position of having to bear witness to Jesus, a position we all find ourselves in sooner or later, we can rely on God's gift of the Spirit. The Spirit of truth will enable us to tell the truth, and people will hear it whether they like it or not.

And we are called (v. 27) to testify. The disciples must tell the world what they have seen and heard, having been with Jesus from the beginning. We in our day testify in the power of the Spirit because of all that we have seen and heard of Jesus, not just in the Gospels but through the many other 'greater works' than his done in his name, whether by St Francis or Mother Teresa or whomever. A new form of life has been let loose in the world. No doubt we are very imperfect witnesses to it. But we glimpse it, we taste it, we see it, and by God's grace we are sometimes able to partake in it. As we do so, we are confronting the world with the love of God.

There is a deep paradox here, because we don't think of love as confrontational, and we often have to learn that to love someone truly may involve confronting them when their way of life is destructive to them or to others. The way of mere tolerance is a very low-grade substitute for true love. Genuine love helps the beloved to see the truth, the way things really are, as Jesus did.

Be close, gracious Lord, to all who today suffer rejection and persecution because they are loyal to your name. Amen.

HOLY WEEK (MONDAY)

JOHN 16:1–11

'I have said these things to you to keep you from stumbling. They will put you out of the synagogues. Indeed, an hour is coming when those who kill you will think that by doing so they are offering worship to God. And they will do this because they have not known the Father or me. But I have said these things to you so that when their hour comes you may remember that I told you about them.

'I did not say these things to you from the beginning, because I was with you. But now I am going to him who sent me; yet none of you asks me, "Where are you going?" But because I have said these things to you, sorrow has filled your hearts. Nevertheless, I tell you the truth: it is to your advantage that I go away, for if I do not go away, the Advocate will not come to you; but if I go, I will send him to you. And when he comes, he will prove the world wrong about sin and righteousness and judgement: about sin, because they do not believe in me; about righteousness, because I am going to the Father and you will see me no longer; about judgement, because the ruler of this world has been condemned.'

Jesus has begun to warn his disciples of what will happen if they follow him. As he says throughout the Gospels, if anyone wants to come after him they must be prepared to take up their cross and follow him. That was more than a metaphor in Jesus' world. Crosses were a routine method of keeping the population in a state of fear, and nobody who had seen a crucifixion would willingly risk going that way themselves. But Jesus says that that is precisely what they must do.

Even before the opposition from Roman officials, however, they will run into hostility from their fellow Jews. Jesus warns them (v. 2) that they will be put out of the synagogues. Although this seems not to have happened until the end of the first century, there were plenty of moves afoot during Jesus' lifetime to have him labelled as a false prophet and thus not only banned from the synagogue but even put to death. Here Jesus warns that the hour is coming when those who kill them will think that by doing so they are offering worship to God. Very shortly after Jesus' resurrection and ascension, Saul of Tarsus was hotly pursuing the early church, believing passionately that by taking them to prison and having them executed he was being loyal to God and zealous for God's law. He, like so many other persecutors, was acting in ignorance of what God is actually like, what he is really doing. Paul says in Romans 10:2 that they have a zeal for God, but it is not according to knowledge (clearly describing his own state before conversion). But Jesus tells his disciples these things (v. 4) so that when the hard times come, they will remember and be confident that they have not taken a false step along the way. They will realize, rather, that the steps they have taken are in the footsteps of Jesus himself.

As the disciples realize that Jesus is leaving them, their hearts grow heavy and sorrowful (v. 6). He still has to explain to them that ultimately it is to their advantage that he goes away, because it is only when he is gone that the Advocate, the Holy Spirit, will come.

Above all else, the disciples need the Spirit in his work as Advocate so that they can witness to the world, testifying to where it has gone wrong. The world is wrong, Jesus says in verse 8, about sin, about righteousness and about judgment. Although the world has some vague ideas about sin, the disciples, by the witness of their lives and the power of the Spirit, must show that the most fundamental thing wrong is that the world has looked at Jesus and rejected him. The world likewise has the wrong idea about who will be vindicated by God. The view of the world in general is that 'the Lord helps those who help themselves', which some people assume is in the Bible. More seriously, the Jews of Jesus' day assumed that God would vindicate all those who were Jewish. Far from it, Jesus says in verse 10. The disciples will bear witness to the fact that Jesus is going to the Father—he is the one who will be vindicated on behalf of them all.

Finally, the world is wrong about judgment. The world thinks that judgment is what happens when the one with the most political or military might condemns those who defy him. On the contrary, says Jesus (v. 11): the witness that you will bear to me in the power of the Spirit will show that the ruler of this world has himself been judged. And here we understand 'the ruler of this world' to mean both the present political structures and the dark spiritual forces that stand behind them. The church must declare by its very existence that there is a different way of being human: a way that owes nothing to the rulers of this world, but everything to the Father who has sent the Son to glorify his name.

Glorify your name, Father, as we bear witness to you before the world. Amen.

HOLY WEEK (TUESDAY)

JOHN 16:12–24

'I still have many things to say to you, but you cannot bear them now. When the Spirit of truth comes, he will guide you into all the truth; for he will not speak on his own, but will speak whatever he hears, and he will declare to you the things that are to come. He will glorify me, because he will take what is mine and declare it to you. All that the Father has is mine. For this reason I said that he will take what is mine and declare it to you.

'A little while, and you will no longer see me, and again a little while, and you will see me.' Then some of his disciples said to one another, 'What does he mean by saying to us, "A little while, and you will no longer see me, and again a little while, and you will see me"; and "Because I am going to the Father"?' They said, 'What does he mean by this "a little while"? We do not know what he is talking about.' Jesus knew that they wanted to ask him, so he said to them, 'Are you discussing among yourselves what I meant when I said, "A little while, and you will no longer see me, and again a little while, and you will see me"? Very truly, I tell you, you will weep and mourn, but the world will rejoice; you will have pain, but your pain will turn into joy. When a woman is in labour, she has pain, because her hour has come. But when her child is born, she no longer remembers the anguish because of the joy of having brought a human being into the world. So you have pain now; but I will see you again, and your hearts will rejoice, and no one will take your joy from you. On that day you will ask nothing of me. Very truly, I tell you, if you ask anything of the Father in my name, he will give it to you. Until now you have not asked for anything in my name. Ask and you will receive, so that your joy may be complete.'

By now, the disciples must have been thoroughly bemused. Not only had Jesus reworked the words of the Passover meal, not only had he washed their feet, but he was now giving them such strange teaching. He was saying that it was God's will for him to go away, and then send the Spirit to them, so that they could continue, without his visible presence, the work that he had been doing.

To reassure them (vv. 12 and 13) he explains that, even though they cannot understand everything that he wants to say to them, the Spirit of truth will come and guide them into all the truth. This is one of the great promises by which the church stands or falls. The church can only continue to exist if it believes that the Spirit is present, leading us into the truth while we struggle to hold onto the love of Jesus and his revelation of God's glory. As verse 13 makes clear, it is the Spirit's task to elucidate what he hears from God, not to bring a fresh revelation himself. We glimpse a picture here of the inner council of God—Father, Son and Spirit—joined together in true harmony of will and love, and the Spirit emerging from that harmony to convey to us the truth of God. All that the Father has belongs to Jesus, and all that is to do with Jesus is now given to the Spirit. Those in whose hearts the Spirit takes up residence have the awesome responsibility of learning from him the truth of God. This should never make us arrogant, although sometimes theologians and others seem to have become so because we do not have to invent or discover these ideas for ourselves. The process takes place as we learn to love one another, to live the life of Christ in and for the world, with the Spirit indwelling us, all the while surprising us with fresh vistas of God's truth.

From verse 16 onwards, Jesus returns to warning the disciples. He has to go away: 'A little while, and you will no longer see me, and again a little while, and you will see me.' The disciples are bewildered, and John, with another touch of comedy, reports the conversation going to and fro like a ping-pong match. What does he mean by 'a little while... and again a little while'? What is this 'little while'? What is he talking about? Jesus seems almost to tease their incomprehension: Is this what you are discussing among yourselves? That I said, 'A little while and this', and 'a little while and that'? He then makes one of the most profound statements in the whole of the farewell discourses (vv. 20–22): 'Very truly, I tell you, you will weep and mourn, but the world will rejoice; you will have pain, but your pain will turn into joy.' The language is almost Pauline: Paul certainly tells a similar story in Romans 8, where the world is in travail, but out of that travail comes God's new creation.

In verse 21 Jesus uses exactly the same image: 'When a woman is in labour, she has pain, because her hour has come. But when her child is born, she no longer remembers the anguish, because of the joy of having brought a human being into the world.' The following verse goes to the very heart of Jesus' vocation to his disciples, then as now. Yes, there is sorrow, but Jesus has promised that beyond the sorrow there is a fresh revelation of himself, his love, his glory. And with that will go a joy that nobody can take away. On that day (v. 23), as he says, they can ask anything of the Father in his name, and he will give it to them. As we have seen, this is one of the repeated themes of the farewell discourses. Through Jesus' achievement, defeating on the cross the ruler of the world, the way is open for his followers, however humbly, however inarticulately, to come before the Father with their requests, knowing that they will be heard and answered. He challenges them, then, in verse 24: 'Until now you have not asked for anything in my name. Ask and you will receive, so that your joy may be complete.'

There are times when the church has taken this challenge seriously. God has then surprised and astonished the church and the world by what he has done through the prayers of faithful people. Sometimes we don't see our prayers answered in the way that we would like. Sometimes we have to come to terms with God's gentle but firm denial of our request, even when we do not understand why. We tend too often, perhaps, to avoid the risk and embarrassment of God saying 'no', and do not even bother to ask. This shows that we have not actually grasped the trinitarian nature of Christian prayer. As we saw in Romans 8, so we see here: we are summoned to a way of life in which God the Father forms the life of Christ in us through the Spirit. Through the Spirit, the Father calls all of us, all his children, to pray; because he has called for these prayers, he will listen and respond to them. As we take part in that inner conversation between God and God, the conversation that happens when we are suffering and rejoicing by turns and sometimes simultaneously, we can be assured that our prayers are heard before the throne of grace. Ask and you will receive, that your joy may be complete.

Help us, Father, to hold on to your promise of joy the other side of sorrow, and meanwhile to pray boldly and faithfully in Jesus' name. Amen.

HOLY WEEK (WEDNESDAY)

JOHN 16:25–33

'I have said these things to you in figures of speech. The hour is coming when I will no longer speak to you in figures, but will tell you plainly of the Father. On that day you will ask in my name. I do not say to you that I will ask the Father on your behalf; for the Father himself loves you, because you have loved me and have believed that I came from God. I came from the Father and have come into the world; again, I am leaving the world and am going to the Father.'

His disciples said, 'Yes, now you are speaking plainly, not in any figure of speech! Now we know that you know all things, and do not need to have anyone question you; by this we believe that you came from God.' Jesus answered them, 'Do you now believe? The hour is coming, indeed it has come, when you will be scattered, each one to his home, and you will leave me alone. Yet I am not alone because the Father is with me. I have said this to you, so that in me you may have peace. In the world you face persecution. But take courage; I have conquered the world!'

Having assured his disciples of the joy and victory awaiting them on the other side of suffering, Jesus now increases that assurance: because they are his people, they are beloved by the Father (v. 27). This is another theme that extends back to the Old Testament, this time to the book of Deuteronomy, when God told the children of Israel through Moses why he had chosen them. It was not because they were particularly strong, or clever, or numerous. It was simply because the Lord loved them and had a purpose through them for the world.

And now Jesus tells them that the time is coming when he will no longer use figures of speech, but speak to them plainly. The Father himself loves them, because they have believed that Jesus came from him. In their response to Jesus they have been responding to God, even if they were no more than dimly aware of that. And by that response, they are gathered into the love of God. As Jesus contemplates leaving the world and returning to the Father, he knows he has accomplished his mission. Through his presence, through his life, and supremely through his death, the Father's glory has been revealed. Those who have seen Jesus and have responded to him in faith and hope and love have been caught up into this great movement. They in turn are now sent into the world by Jesus to accomplish the work he has set them.

The disciples are clearly delighted to have Jesus speaking in a more straightforward fashion (v. 29). 'Now we know,' they say, 'that you truly know all things.' They have watched people quizzing Jesus and putting hard questions to him in the temple. They have watched the doctors of the law trying to catch him out on tricky points. And now they see that this was all unnecessary. There is a level that leaves nit-picking and angry discourse behind. Thomas Aquinas wrote the wonderful *Summa Theologica*, brilliantly explaining the whole of Christianity, but, towards the end of his life, he received a fresh vision of God, granted to him personally, that made everything else look like so much straw. In a similar way, the disciples see that all their anxious puzzling, trying to fit Jesus into existing categories, was beside the point. Now they have a revelation of the life and glory of God that transcends such questioning. Jesus has come from God to express his love; he is returning in triumph to the Father, and leaving them with the Spirit to carry on the work.

Jesus does not, however, give them the impression that they can now rest in this knowledge. On the contrary, if they do believe in him, that belief is now going to be tested to the uttermost (v. 32). The hour is coming, within a matter of minutes, when they will be scattered, each one to his own home, and they will leave him alone. Jesus must accomplish his final work alone. The disciples are caught in the tension between what Jesus will work through them in the future, and the situation they face in the present when they are about to be left behind for a few days by what God must do through Jesus alone. And yet he will not be alone, because the Father is with him. He is with him not just in the sense of accompanying him, reassuring him, strengthening him as he goes to the cross, but in the sense that the Father is expressing his own love through him. What Jesus is about to do on the cross will be incomprehensible to the disciples—and even more so to the world—but it is the perfect expression of the Father's love.

Jesus finishes his great discourse with a final reassurance: he has told them all this so that they may have peace, despite the persecution and tribulation that they will face. Again we find the words of this gospel very similar to Paul at the end of Romans 8: despite nakedness, peril, or sword, 'in all these things we are more than conquerors through him who loved us'. Jesus says here (v. 33), 'In the world you face persecution. But take courage; I have conquered the world!' In a sense Jesus knows that the work has already been accomplished. He will declare on the cross, 'It is finished!' But here, in the upper room, he sees the end from the beginning, and can tell the disciples that he has overcome the world. Although the world will trouble them, although it will throw all kinds of evil at them, yet they can be of good cheer. Jesus has granted them peace.

Father, grant to us such a vision of your glory and truth as will go beyond all argument and sustain us through all suffering. Amen.

Holy Week (Maundy Thursday)

John 17:1–5

After Jesus had spoken these words, he looked up to heaven and said, 'Father, the hour has come; glorify your Son so that the Son may glorify you, since you have given him authority over all people, to give eternal life to all whom you have given him. And this is eternal life, that they may know you, the only true God, and Jesus Christ whom you have sent. I glorified you on earth by finishing the work that you gave me to do. So now, Father, glorify me in your own presence with the glory that I had in your presence before the world existed.'

We now turn to what has become known as the 'great high priestly prayer'. Jesus takes upon himself the task that had always been the high priest's task: interceding on behalf of the people of God. In this case he prays for his own disciples and the spreading network of others who would come to believe through their work. On this Maundy Thursday, as we reflect on Jesus' farewell to his followers, we see it in terms of Jesus as the priest, standing between the Father and the rest of us. He is the one through whom the love of God flows to us, and through whom, astonishingly, our response of love to the Father flows back again in gratitude. Jesus draws together in this prayer all the work that he has done—walking through Galilean villages, preaching the kingdom, healing the sick, celebrating the kingdom with outcasts and outsiders, confronting the self-appointed guardians of Israel's traditions, and coming to Jerusalem, as Messiah, to complete his God-given work.

As he starts this prayer, he looks up to heaven with the words (v. 1): 'Father, the hour has come.' We have already seen from John 12 that Jesus knew the hour had come when the Greeks came to the feast and sought to see him. We were reminded at the beginning of John 13 of how Jesus knew that his hour had come to depart from the world and return to the Father. And now he says to his Father that the hour has indeed come. At the heart of the whole prayer is the request that the Father will glorify the Son so that the Son may glorify the Father. That is to say, that God will so act now, at this moment, through Jesus, that Jesus himself may be exalted, lifted up on the cross to draw all people to himself. Jesus asks this so that he may complete the work for which he came into the world, thereby bringing glory to God. It is the quintessence of Jesus' prayer, and perhaps of any prayer, that the Father would work to glorify his name in the world, so that the deeds of his people, specifically in this case his Son, will in turn bring him glory.

Jesus knows that, as the Messiah, he has been given authority (v. 2). If we read back in the Old Testament, in the Psalms and in the prophets, we find again and again that when God finally sends his true anointed king, this king will have dominion from one sea to another, from the Great River to the ends of the earth. Jesus is aware of his vocation to be Israel's Messiah, not in the way that Israel had thought, but in the way that God had designed from all eternity. And the Messiah comes in order to bring to birth the new age for which Israel has longed. Israel laboured long in what they called the old age, the present age, and they longed for the new age to be born, which they called 'the age to come'. We rather unhappily translate the relevant Greek phrase as 'eternal life', and we are easily misled into thinking that eternal life has nothing to do with the old Jewish expectation. For us, 'eternal life' tends to mean escaping from space and time into a different realm altogether, an idea that bears no relation to the Jewish thought of Jesus and the writer of this gospel.

As Messiah, Jesus has authority not only to inaugurate the age to come but to take into that new age all those whom God has given him. So what will this new age look like? It will begin with Jesus dying the death which is the final seal on Israel's exile, then bursting from the grave to be the beginning of God's new creation. All those who know him will, through him, come to know God himself, and we must remind ourselves here that the verb 'to know' in the Bible has much deeper and more intimate meaning than in modern English. Belonging to the new age means knowing God, knowing that he is the only true God, and knowing that all other gods are idols. And as children of God's new age, we know that Jesus is the Messiah, sent by God. In verse 4, Jesus moves on to look at what he has done: he has glorified God on earth by finishing the work given him to do. Jesus has a wonderful serenity about him. There were many lepers in Israel who had not been cleansed, many widows whose only sons had died and not been raised to life. There were many poor people still unable to feed themselves, many prisoners yet to be freed. But Jesus has finished the specific work that God gave him. It was not his task to right the world's wrongs overnight. It was his task to confront evil and defeat it; and he had now accomplished this. All that remained was to finish the accomplishment of that work on the cross. Knowing this, he asks his Father to glorify him with the glory that he had in God's presence before the world existed.

I don't think this means that Jesus could, in his human memory, recall a time when he was united in his pre-incarnate existence with the Father and the Holy Spirit, enjoying the relationship of the blessed Trinity. Rather, I believe it to mean that he knew it was his task as Messiah to accomplish upon the earth that which, according to scripture, only the one true God could accomplish. He knew deep within himself that this meant he was the expression, the embodiment, even the incarnation, of the one true God.

The beginning of this prayer is an extraordinary statement of faith and vocation. Jesus is going to the horror of the cross, praying that the God who made the world, the God who called Israel, the God who had called him to be Messiah, would be glorified and would glorify him. This is a prayer that, to begin with, demands that we simply stand back and reflect on it in wonder and awe. Through our reflection, however, and in particular through the celebration of the Eucharist, commemorating Jesus' last supper, we can find ourselves enfolded within the prayer. We can discover ourselves to be the ones for whom Jesus was praying, those who know the only true God and Jesus the Messiah who had been sent by him. As we meditate on him as he makes his way to Gethsemane, to betrayal, to trial, to crucifixion, we watch with love and awe, seeing Jesus glorified in God's presence, and God glorified in him.

Lord Jesus, only Son of the living God, pray for us now, that we may know the Father through knowing you. Amen.

HOLY WEEK (GOOD FRIDAY)

JOHN 17:6–19

'I have made your name known to those whom you gave me from the world. They were yours, and you gave them to me, and they have kept your word. Now they know that everything you have given me is from you; for the words that you gave to me I have given to them, and they have received them and know in truth that I came from you; and they have believed that you sent me. I am asking on their behalf; I am not asking on behalf of the world, but on behalf of those whom you gave me, because they are yours. All mine are yours, and yours are mine; and I have been glorified in them. And now I am no longer in the world, but they are in the world, and I am coming to you. Holy Father, protect them in your name that you have given me, so that they may be one, as we are one. While I was with them, I protected them in your name that you have given me. I guarded them, and not one of them was lost except the one destined to be lost, so that the scripture might be fulfilled. But now I am coming to you, and I speak these things in the world so that they may have my joy made complete in themselves. I have given them your word, and the world has hated them because they do not belong to the world, just as I do not belong to the world. I am not asking you to take them out of the world, but I ask you to protect them from the evil one. They do not belong to the world, just as I do not belong to the world. Sanctify them in the truth; your word is truth. As you have sent me into the world, so I have sent them into the world. And for their sakes I sanctify myself, so that they also may be sanctified in truth.

As we approach Good Friday, the most solemn and deep moment in the whole Christian calendar, we find ourselves in the middle of the prayer that Jesus prayed the night before he died. He has just prayed that God will glorify him, which, as we have seen, is a prayer that through the crucifixion God will reveal himself fully as the one true God, the lover of Israel and the world. Jesus now comes before the Father on behalf of all those whom the Father has given him, and, praying as the great high priest, he prays a prayer of 'sanctification'.

The Hebrew word for 'sanctification' meant that something had been consecrated to God, given over to his use so that it became holy. On the cross, Jesus consecrated himself utterly, gave himself up to the Father's will. He bore in his own body the shame, the failure, the sin, the agony of Israel and of the world, in order to bring them healing and to embody the love of God. It is out of that vocation that he prays for his people, for those sitting around the table with him, for Mary and Martha and Lazarus, for others whose names we do not know—people who had seen a glimpse of God in him and trusted in him, who were now living his way and waiting anxiously for the coming of the kingdom.

To begin with (v. 6), Jesus says to the Father that he has made the Father's name known to these people. We have no record that Jesus taught people a totally new name for God. Jews had already called God 'Father', as far back as the days of the Exodus. But Jesus has made known to his people the inner character of God, God's name in the sense of who God really is. He has revealed the Father perfectly, as one who is infinitely tender, strong to heal, gentle with the wounded, firm to the point of severity with those who blindly oppose his will.

And as he has revealed God's character he has found that God has given him a new chosen people, the people through whom he will now bless the world. God has chosen them as he chose Israel, and has given them to Jesus. And as he says (v. 7), they know and trust that everything that God has given to him is truly from God. Jesus has given them the words God gave to him, and they have received these words as truth. They have come to believe with all their hearts that God sent Jesus to them. Throughout the farewell discourses we have seen how Peter, Thomas, Philip and Judas (not Judas Iscariot) had still been puzzled, muddled, questioning. But they had enough faith to be there, enough faith to cling on to Jesus, forsaking all other paths, all other leaders. They had clung on in faith despite their lack of understanding, believing that Jesus was indeed the one that God had sent. Therefore Jesus is praying for them (v. 9), that by the power of the Spirit, his work would continue through them to touch the whole world. He celebrates the fact that God has given them to him (v. 10), seeing that he is already in one sense glorified in them, because he has established them as the new Israel.

This is part of the confirmation of his messianic mission. He prays (v. 11) that God will protect these little ones, these disciples, muddled, misguided, and yet faithful followers. Under the protection of God, they will be one, as God and Jesus are one.

Jesus then looks back to his ministry among them (v. 12): 'While I was with them, I protected them in your name... I guarded them, and not one of them was lost except the one destined to be lost, so that the scripture might be fulfilled.' And in verses 13 and 14, he bequeaths his joy to his followers. As we saw earlier, the promise of joy is accompanied by the warning that the world hates the people of God. Those who follow Jesus are bound to seem out of step with the world, which organizes itself according to power and prestige, wealth and human status. On his way to the cross, Jesus is turning all that upside-down, and knows that just as the world hated him, so those who follow him will be hated. He therefore prays (v. 15) that they may be protected from the evil one. They will not only be protected, however. Like Jesus, they are to be set aside for God's use (v. 17), sanctified in the truth that is God's word.

As God sent Jesus into the world, so Jesus is now sending his followers into the world. We can imagine that, as his followers listened to this prayer, and then saw Jesus go to his trial and his shameful death, they could not begin to understand how they could have any mission to the world at all. Yet Jesus, on the night that he was betrayed, sees that through the cross he will defeat evil, thus enabling his people to receive the Spirit and be sent out into the world. As Jesus goes to the cross, he prays for his faithful ones that, as he has been sanctified, so may all those who truly know him be sanctified in the truth. On this Good Friday Jesus' prayer reaches out to enfold all of us who kneel at the foot of the cross. We come here not in order to boost our own spirituality, but to be consecrated to the will of God, so that the work of God, uniquely accomplished in Jesus, may now be implemented through us.

Help us, Lord Jesus, so to watch and wait with you this day; that, as you loved us to the end, so we may remain faithful to you, and through you be consecrated to the Father's service. Amen.

Holy Week (Holy Saturday)

John 17:20–26

'I ask not only on behalf of these, but also on behalf of those who will believe in me through their word, that they may all be one. As you, Father, are in me and I am in you, may they also be in us, so that the world may believe that you have sent me. The glory that you have given me I have given them, so that they may be one, as we are one, I in them and you in me, that they may become completely one, so that the world may know that you have sent me and have loved them even as you have loved me. Father, I desire that those also, whom you have given me, may be with me where I am, to see my glory, which you have given me because you loved me before the foundation of the world.

'Righteous Father, the world does not know you, but I know you; and these know that you have sent me. I made your name known to them, and I will make it known, so that the love with which you have loved me may be in them, and I in them.'

Holy Saturday is a day of silence. Jesus has finished the work that he was given to do. Now, like the Father in Genesis chapter 1, after the six days of creation, he rests. God rests in Christ in the tomb, awaiting the dawning of the new creation on Easter morning. And into that silence we take the conclusion of Jesus' final prayer. Now it is more than a prayer for his immediate followers. It is a prayer for those who, through the work and witness of those followers, will in time come to believe. As part of his messianic vocation, Jesus knew that it was his task to accomplish something that would resonate out into all creation. In this way the whole world would know that the God of all the earth was indeed the God of Israel, who had fulfilled his plan to defeat the evil corrupting the world, through his anointed king and Messiah, Jesus.

As the great high priest, Jesus prays for those who will one day join the company of his followers. Once again we can imagine the puzzled faces of Peter, James and John and the others around the table. Their plan for Jesus to become king of Israel had been very different. Nothing had turned out as they had supposed. Little do they know that they have an even worse shock in store on the next day, when they will see their master crucified. They still do not fully realize that this is the way in which they will be equipped as his heralds, ambassadors of the king, to go out into all the world.

So what does Jesus pray for the larger gathering of followers, those who will come to believe in him through the word of his disciples, including you and me today? He prays that they may all be one (v. 21). As we look around at the church today, we have to admit that this part of his prayer is still awaiting its full answer. From the very beginning the church struggled to maintain a difficult unity between Hebrews and Hellenists. There were divisions and arguments about what was proper and what was not proper as the church's mission spread. There were moments of unity, but also moments of terrible division. And we, twenty centuries later, have seen even greater divisions—between east and west, between Catholic and Protestant, rich and poor, black and white, north and south.

On this Holy Saturday, as we find ourselves enfolded in the prayer of Jesus, reflecting on the shame of the cross and the grave of our Lord, we should pray and seek once more for the humility to say that all those who find salvation in Jesus Christ are our brothers and sisters. We should commit ourselves once more to finding ways of expressing that family relationship as fully as we can. It is no cheap or superficial unity that we seek: in verse 21 Jesus prays that the unity of his people may reflect and embody the unity that he had with the Father. It is a prayer that God will send his Spirit upon his people, to bind them into the inner life of the Trinity, with the result that the world will see and then believe. As it is, the world looks at the divisions in the church and mocks the differences between ideal and reality. If Christians came together across traditional barriers, even occasionally, the world would indeed see a different way of life, a way of glory, a way of love. Jesus has given (v. 22) the very glory of God to his followers, so that we may be one. We, the church, must embody the God-ness of God, the self-giving love of God (v. 23): 'I in them and you in me, that they may become completely one.'

And in this way the world will know love. Most of the time people can easily belittle love, explaining it away as selfish, self-interested, mercenary. They find it hard to believe that there is such a thing as utter self-giving love, that it is, in fact, the strongest force in the world. Jesus longs that his people may be immersed in this love, and so be able to share it with others. The love between God the Father and his Son is the most unique and precious thing in the world. It is the force through which the world was made, the force through which it is redeemed, as we solemnly celebrate this weekend. The power of this love is now to be let loose in the world through those for whom Jesus has prayed.

In verses 25 and 26, the prayer comes to its still, central conclusion: at the moment the world does not know God, although Jesus knows God, and his followers know that Jesus was sent by God. Jesus has made God's name known to his followers, and will continue to make it known, as he pours out his Spirit on them. In this way, the love with which God has loved Jesus will be in them; through the presence and power of the Holy Spirit, Jesus himself will be in them. They will bring glory to God by witnessing to the world that there is a different way, the way of love, the way of self-giving.

As we observe this Holy Saturday with still, patient hearts, let us join our own prayers with that of Jesus. Let us pray that he will be glorified through our witness. Above all, may we, with all God's people, find a way to be one, so that the world may believe. Our vocation is nothing less than this, whatever it costs. This is how God will be glorified, and how it will be known that he has loved Jesus, and in loving Jesus has loved us, and in loving us has loved the world.

Father, may all your people be one, as you and Jesus are one. Show us the way to true unity, so that the world may believe. Amen.

WEEK 8 (EASTER SUNDAY)

1 CORINTHIANS 15:1—11

Now I should remind you, brothers and sisters, of the good news that I proclaimed to you, which you in turn received, in which also you stand, through which also you are being saved, if you hold firmly to the message that I proclaimed to you—unless you have come to believe in vain.

For I handed on to you as of first importance what I in turn had received: that Christ died for our sins in accordance with the scriptures, and that he was buried, and that he was raised on the third day in accordance with the scriptures, and that he appeared to Cephas, then to the twelve. Then he appeared to more than five hundred brothers and sisters at one time, most of whom are still alive, though some have died. Then he appeared to James, then to all the apostles. Last of all, as to someone untimely born, he appeared also to me. For I am the least of the apostles, unfit to be called an apostle, because I persecuted the church of God. But by the grace of God I am what I am, and his grace towards me has not been in vain. On the contrary, I worked harder than any of them—though it was not I, but the grace of God that is with me. Whether then it was I or they, so we proclaim and so you have come to believe.

As Easter morning breaks we go back to one of the very earliest parts of the New Testament. Not that it was written down at the very beginning; but Paul, in writing 1 Corinthians 15, begins his long exposition of Easter by quoting the earliest tradition that we have on the subject. Paul had previously given to the Corinthians a summary of what Christians believed; that summary, as we shall see, focuses on the resurrection of Jesus from the dead.

Paul deals with many different issues in 1 Corinthians, several of which have to do with the Corinthians' mistaken desire to attain some sort of super-spirituality. They wanted to attain in the present life such a fulness of God's blessing that it would leave no room for the resurrection of the body as a further gift of God. At the climax of the letter, then, Paul sets out an extensive discussion of Easter and all that it means, to bring them firmly back on track.

He begins with a reminder of the gospel message, the good news that he proclaimed to them from the beginning. This is the message by which they should stand firm, by which they are saved (v. 2)—so as long as they hold it firm. And, beginning in verse 3 and continuing at least to verse 7, Paul expounds the fact that the Messiah, the Christ, died for their sins in accordance with the scriptures. It is in Jesus, as Messiah, that God's plan to deal with the sins of the world through Israel has reached its triumphant conclusion. When he says that this took place in accordance with the scriptures, he does not mean a few convenient proof texts. He means that the drama and narrative of the entire scriptural record reached its climax when Jesus died on the cross.

The next element of the message that, as we shall see, is very important for Paul, is that Jesus was buried (v. 4). His body was not left on the cross to rot, as many crucified bodies were, but was taken down and buried. It is interesting to note that when Paul, as a Pharisee, spoke of resurrection he meant far more than 'life after death' in some generalized or non-physical sense. The Jews of Paul's day believed many different things about what happened to people after their death, but the Pharisees believed in resurrection. They believed that God gave people a new, or renewed, body after their death. When, therefore, Paul says that Jesus was raised on the third day, having been buried, and that this happened in accordance with the scriptures, he does not mean that Jesus now has a wonderful spiritualized existence beyond the earthly sphere. He means that God's new age has begun, that the time foretold by the prophets has come at last.

He knows that Jesus was raised from the dead, and he knows it because certain people (including himself) saw the risen Jesus. He appeared to Cephas (that is the Aramaic word for Peter) and then to the twelve disciples. Although Paul mentions twelve of them here, we have no reason to suppose that Jesus appeared to Judas Iscariot. Paul's phrase shows, however, that 'the twelve' was fixed in the earliest tradition, because it also indicated that they were representatives of the New Israel, through whom the message would now go out to the world. Then, says Paul (v. 6), Jesus appeared to more than five hundred Christians at one time, most of whom were still alive. Clearly, he is telling the Corinthians that there are a good many witnesses of the risen Jesus who would vouch for what Paul is saying. Jesus also appeared to James—not one of the twelve, but the Lord's brother. This James had not been a believer during Jesus' own lifetime, but came to faith when Jesus appeared to him, and was very quickly established as a key leader of the early church. And Jesus appeared to the whole company of his apostles: for Paul, an 'apostle' was, quite simply, one who had seen the risen Lord.

At the end, Paul describes his own conversion. He uses very interesting language to describe what happened to him. He says first (v. 8) that he was 'last of all'. In other words, when Paul saw the risen Jesus, it was more than the kind of spiritual experience that subsequent Christians have had. People sometimes say that we know Christ is risen because of his presence with us today. Of course that is part of the evidence for the resurrection, but Paul had the unique experience of seeing the risen Jesus, something vouchsafed to only a few. The Corinthians had had every other kind of Christian spiritual experience imaginable, but they had not seen the risen Jesus with their own eyes. When Paul describes his experience, however, he uses a phrase which shows it was a very different experience from the encounters of Cephas, James and the others who had seen the risen Lord. He says (v. 8) that it happened to him 'as to one untimely born'. We should perhaps translate that more vividly. The Greek phrase means 'as to one ripped from the womb, born by a sudden Caesarean section'. It is a very violent image for Paul to use. It must indicate Paul's memory of the time when a sudden, dazzling light and a shocking, new revelation burst upon him so that he was stunned, blinded, and could hardly breathe, let alone speak. This was God's extraordinary way of turning him from being a persecutor to being an apostle.

As he says in verses 9, 10 and 11, he was the least of all the apostles, unfit even to be called an apostle, because he had been persecuting the church of God. He had seen the early Christian movement as a dire threat to Judaism and all that it represented. He thought that if people started believing in Jesus, it would undo all the work that he, as a Pharisee, was desperately trying to do, to make Israel fit for the coming kingdom of God. On the road to

Damascus he had to realize that he was the one at fault, that it was he who had got everything upside-down. It was only by the grace of God (v. 10) that he had become what he was. As a result of God's grace, he then worked harder than all the other apostles, putting all his God-given energy into the task. In verse 11, he rounds off his initial statement of the gospel. What he has preached, and what all the other apostles have preached, is basically the same message: the death and resurrection of the Messiah, accomplishing God's plan for the salvation of the world. This plan, prepared ages ago, was announced through the whole story of Israel, and reached its glorious completion in the resurrection of Jesus from the dead. People often talk about early Christians living in the last days, awaiting the second coming. In a sense that's true, but it misses the most important point. From Paul's perspective, he was living in the first days of God's new world.

Since Jesus had been raised from the dead, the new world had dawned. From now on, everything was going to be different.

We thank you, gracious God, that in Jesus' death and resurrection you fulfilled your plan to save the world. Amen.

WEEK 8 (EASTER MONDAY)

I CORINTHIANS 15:12–19

Now if Christ is proclaimed as raised from the dead, how can some of you say there is no resurrection of the dead? If there is no resurrection of the dead, then Christ has not been raised; and if Christ has not been raised, then our proclamation has been in vain and your faith has been in vain. We are even found to be misrepresenting God, because we testified of God that he raised Christ— whom he did not raise if it is true that the dead are not raised. For if the dead are not raised, then Christ has not been raised. If Christ has not been raised, your faith is futile and you are still in your sins. Then those also who have died in Christ have perished. If for this life only we have hoped in Christ, we are of all people most to be pitied.

Having set out the gospel that he and the other disciples had preached from the beginning, Paul turns to the specific question that the Corinthians seemed to be raising. Some of them were saying that there could be no resurrection of the dead; as we saw yesterday, they may well have been people who thought they had already attained such a level of spirituality that any possible 'resurrection' had already taken place, perhaps at their baptism, or perhaps when God gave them the Holy Spirit. They were already new people, already exalted to share the heavenly throne of Christ.

Paul does not deny the new life that they claim in faith through baptism and the gift of the Spirit. But, at the same time, in a profound and powerful sense, the resurrection of the dead is yet to come. Paul begins this argument by pointing out that if there is no resurrection of the dead, then Christ has not been raised. If all he had needed was a life of super-spirituality, he would not have needed to rise from the tomb. He would have reached all possible spiritual heights before his death. If Christ has not been raised, however (v. 14), then what Paul has been preaching, and what they have believed, is rubbish. The Christian gospel announced in

Corinth was not simply a message about a new sort of spirituality, a new level of spiritual attainment to which people could aspire. The message was about an event in world history, as a result of which a new day had dawned, foreshadowing the dawning of God's final, eternal day.

Paul continues his reasoning in verse 15: if it is true that there is no such thing as actual physical resurrection, then he has been misrepresenting God. He has been preaching that God raised the Messiah from the dead, and, if such things never happen, he is attributing to God something that he did not do. And if the dead are not raised (v. 16) then the Messiah has not been raised. If the Messiah has not been raised (v. 17) the faith of the Corinthians is futile, and they are still in their sins. Paul does not see salvation in terms of a new level of spirituality, but as something that God has done within history. To understand this, we must return to the Jewish world-view from which Paul started and in which he continued as a Christian.

As a Christian, Paul never stopped thinking Jewishly. He presented a Jewish message for the whole world. For him, salvation from sin was not merely a personal matter to be applied to each individual. Of course it was that, too, but only because it was first something much larger. It was God's plan that the shame and pain of the world would devolve on to Israel, his people, while they languished in exile because of their sins. It would then devolve on to the Messiah, in order that sin might be dealt with through his death. How do we know that Jesus was the true Messiah? We know that in him God fulfilled his purpose for Israel, that of dealing with the sin of the world. We only know that Jesus as Messiah defeated sin, if we know that he defeated death itself. The resurrection, therefore, demonstrates that Jesus was who he claimed to be, the one who brought Israel's destiny to its climax, who dealt with the sin of the world. If the Messiah has not been raised, the Corinthians are still in their pre-Christian state. Nothing significant has happened to them. They cannot celebrate God's forgiveness, the coming of his new age, the gift of the Spirit, unless the resurrection has occurred.

Two other things follow from this, set out in verses 18 and 19. Firstly, if it is true that the Messiah has not been raised from the dead, then, as far as Paul is concerned, there is no future for those who have belonged to Christ in this life and who have now died. They have perished forever, and can no longer share the resurrection life. Secondly, if it is true that the resurrection has not happened, and indeed will not happen, then those apostles who have endured persecution and hardship on behalf of the Messiah are fools. They are 'of all people most to be pitied', if there is no future hope. In this paragraph, therefore, Paul goes straight to the heart of the problem. In effect, he tells the Corinthians that anybody denying the future resurrection of the dead must realize that there are in fact no other options for Christian believers. If it is not true that the Messiah rose from the dead, then all else is undermined, all the benefits that they claim to enjoy as Christians: forgiveness of sins, the assurance of reunion with loved ones who have died, and the whole point of their work in the present time.

We still need to remind ourselves today that the resurrection remains the foundation of all Christian existence. Without the resurrection, we are simply left with another variation on the general religious themes that circulate the world. With the resurrection we believe, with Paul, that the new day has dawned. God's new creation has begun.

Help us, Father, so to grasp the truth of Jesus' resurrection that our whole life may be a witness to your new creation. Amen.

WEEK 8 (TUESDAY)

1 CORINTHIANS 15:20—28

But in fact Christ has been raised from the dead, the first fruits of those who have died. For since death came through a human being, the resurrection of the dead has also come through a human being; for as all die in Adam, so all will be made alive in Christ. But each in his own order: Christ the first fruits, then at his coming those who belong to Christ. Then comes the end, when he hands over the kingdom to God the Father, after he has destroyed every ruler and every authority and power. For he must reign until he has put all his enemies under his feet. The last enemy to be destroyed is death. For 'God has put all things in subjection under his feet.' But when it says, 'All things are put in subjection', it is plain that this does not include the one who put all things in subjection under him. When all things are subjected to him, then the Son himself will also be subjected to the one who put all things in subjection under him, so that God may be all in all.

Paul has laid the groundwork for his central exposition of how the resurrection of Jesus fits into the overall plan of God. He has reminded the Corinthians clearly and sharply of the basic gospel message. He has warned them that if they think the promised resurrection is an optional extra, they are actually undermining all that they believe as Christians. Now he begins to explain to them how the resurrection of Jesus was the initial climax of God's purposes, which will reach final fulfilment in the resurrection of all God's people. In fact, he says in verse 20, Christ has been raised from the dead as 'the first fruits of those who have fallen asleep', using this gentle phrase 'falling asleep' as a way of pointing to the 'awakening' after death that is yet to come.

He continues by putting Christ and Adam alongside one another (vv. 21–22). As death came through a human being, so the resurrection of the dead has come through a human being: '...for as all die in Adam, so all will be made alive in Christ.' As God made creation in the beginning, so now God is remaking creation. Just as death came into the world through the rebellion of the human race, so now Jesus as a human being has defeated death and brought the promise of new life. Paul then goes on to explain the difference between the Christian belief and the Jewish belief in this matter. Many Jews, and no doubt Paul himself, had believed that when the Messiah came he would usher in a new age at once. There would be no overlap period. The Messiah would establish the kingdom of God, raise the dead, make everything new, all overnight. What has happened instead, as Paul grasps, is that God's purposes are being fulfilled in a two-stage process, rather than a single act. The resurrection of Jesus the Messiah is like the first part of the harvest (v. 23), the first fruits of the crop, which were brought into the temple at Jerusalem as a thanksgiving to God and as the assurance of the great harvest still to come.

This image of the first fruits enables Paul to explain how the resurrection of Jesus was the beginning of the end, and that there is more of the end yet to come, with the resurrection of all Jesus' people.

So what will this final end look like? It will be the time, at the end of the present mode of history, when Jesus, already ruling over the world as the exalted human Lord, completes his work and hands over the kingdom to God the Father. Every ruler, authority and power that has defied God's kingdom will be destroyed. Their power is kept intact by the threat of death; how can they keep their authority if death itself is destroyed? The Prince of Peace will therefore 'reign until he has put all his enemies under his feet' (v. 25). Paul is quoting here from Psalm 110, a prediction of the coming of God's king, the Messiah.

In verse 26, he says that the last enemy to be destroyed is death. Christians sometimes pretend that death is no longer an enemy, that maybe it is even a friend. Some great saints, such as St Francis, have seen a sense in which death can be a kindness, a gentle act of God in putting to sleep a beloved child at the end of a long and weary life, in the hope of the glorious awakening to come. At the same time Paul sees death as an enemy, because the corruption of our present physical body involves the destruction of something good and God-given. The resurrection is essential to both Jewish and Christian thought, because we believe in the goodness of

God's creation, and believe, therefore, that the corruption and decay of this creation is not God's final or most important word. Death is necessary in the present mode of time, but one day God will deal with death itself and bring in his new creation, the re-embodiment of his people. When death is destroyed, God will put all things in subjection under Jesus' feet (v. 27). Here he is quoting from Psalm 8, using a passage which, this time, is not about the Messiah, but about the human race. What has happened in Christ is God's plan not just for God's incarnate self, but for the whole human race. God's intention all along was to rule the world through obedient humanity—but where is such an obedient humanity to be found? Only, at this time, in Jesus himself: because he has been totally obedient to the saving plan of God, he is now set in authority over the world.

In verse 28 Paul draws his argument to its conclusion. When all things are subject to Christ, to the Messiah, then the Son himself will be subjected to God the Father, that God may be all in all. In his own highly typical style, Paul is echoing the great high-priestly prayer that we studied in Holy Week. They both state that what God the Father has accomplished, he has accomplished through the Son. Or, to put it another way, what God the Son has accomplished, he has accomplished as the Father's agent. The work he has done in the world is done as the revelation of the glory and kingdom of God. We would have to say, in fact, that if the doctrine of the Trinity did not exist, it would be necessary, on the basis of 1 Corinthians 15, to invent it, because it is through the Messiah and in his resurrection that God the Creator has fulfilled his promise to make the world over anew.

Paul therefore tells the Corinthians that they find themselves poised between the beginning of the resurrection and the completion of the resurrection. Jesus passed through death, through the grave, and on into a mode of existence never known before, the beginning of God's new creation. Above all, Paul is anxious that the Corinthians should not imagine they have already received everything that God has promised as part of the new creation. If they think that, they will fail to see the glory awaiting them, when God does for them what he has done for Jesus, completing his plan to renew the whole world, to make all things new, so that God may be all in all.

As we celebrate, Lord Jesus, your victory over death, so give us joy in awaiting the renewal of the whole creation. Amen.

Week 8 (Wednesday)

1 Corinthians 15:29–34

Otherwise, what will those people do who receive baptism on behalf of the dead? If the dead are not raised at all, why are people baptized on their behalf?

And why are we putting ourselves in danger every hour? I die every day! That is as certain, brothers and sisters, as my boasting of you—a boast that I make in Christ Jesus our Lord. If with merely human hopes I fought with wild animals at Ephesus, what would I have gained by it? If the dead are not raised, 'Let us eat and drink, for tomorrow we die.' Do not be deceived: 'Bad company ruins good morals.' Come to a sober and right mind, and sin no more; for some people have no knowledge of God. I say this to your shame.

In many of Paul's longer arguments, we find him breaking the logical sequence of thought, perhaps in order to lighten the load for his hearers who, after all, were listening to the letter read aloud, not studying it privately. He would also change tack in order to drive home to them more personally a particular point, before continuing to develop the argument. Here, in verses 29–34, he applies what he has been saying to two particular issues that relate to the themes of verses 18 and 19.

First, he addresses the question of what happens to those who have died. In verse 18 he said that, if there is no future resurrection, then those who have died in Christ have perished utterly. As a Pharisaic Jew, Paul could never be content with envisaging disembodied souls or spirits as the final state of God's people. He believed so passionately in the goodness of God's created world, and the goodness of the human being made in the image of God, that he could not bear the thought of human existence continuing only in some disembodied state.

A practice had been established in the early church whereby those who had become Christians and then died before baptism were honoured by having other people baptized on their behalf.

Their view of baptism seems to have been so strong that they regarded it as vital that even the dead should share in it in some way. They were thereby enfolded within the life of the visible community, even though they had not themselves received the sacrament of baptism. Paul uses this practice as an example to drive home his point: if they do not believe in a future resurrection, why this practice of special baptism? Those people have gone. Even if they are now no more than disembodied souls they will never receive a new life in Christ if the dead are not raised. Today we do not baptize people on behalf of those who have died, but we can understand why that practice developed. And we can see what Paul is forcing the Corinthians to see: that, if there is no future resurrection, this rich, symbolic practice of baptizing people in this way is meaningless.

The second issue that Paul raises re-emphasizes the point made in verse 19: if there is no future resurrection life when God will make all things new, what is the point of his (Paul's) apostolic labours? What is the point of Paul coming into every town knowing that he is liable to be stoned or beaten or put in the stocks or ridiculed? As he says in verse 31, he faces death every day. Every day he faces the little death of ridicule, shame, or persecution, and every day he faces the possibility of actual death, the chance that they may actually set the lions on him, or that a stone thrown by somebody will actually kill him. This daily hardship is as certain as his boasting of them, a boast that he makes in Christ Jesus. In other words, just as he boasts of them, of their faith as Christians, so he knows all too well that every day he must face tribulation and hardship.

As we saw at the beginning of 2 Corinthians, which we studied early in Lent, Paul endured the most terrible time of his life in Ephesus. He says that he fought with wild animals there (v. 32), and some people think that he was actually put in the arena to face combat with wolves, bears or lions. Others think that this is merely metaphorical, but that it was a very vivid metaphor to show what Paul was suffering, perhaps implying that he was battling with the wild beasts of depression, failure, and opposition within the church. He puts to the Corinthians the fact that, without the hope of a future resurrection, he would not put himself through such agony. If the dead are not raised, why bother? Let's eat and drink, for tomorrow we die—a fatalist statement of living as if only this life mattered. And to rub in the point, Paul quotes from the Greek poet Menander (v. 33): 'Bad company ruins good morals.' He points out to them that they can choose the way of mindless indulgence, enjoying however much life they have left. If they do so, though, they must remember that there will be a price to pay. They will ultimately disintegrate as human beings, cease being the people God intended them to be.

He appeals to them, therefore (v. 34): 'Come to a sober and right mind, and sin no more.' He regards their denial of the resurrection as missing the mark—and that is what sin means. If they think that they already have all the future life that God has for them, they are deeply deceived. Living the way they are, thinking the thoughts that they do, they are failing in their task of bringing the gospel of Jesus to the world.

In this short and, to us, rather strange passage, Paul rigorously applies his teaching about the future resurrection: if the resurrection is not true, then there is no hope for those who have died, and no point to the work of the living. By clarifying these vital points, Paul prepares the way for the next stage of his argument, to which we shall turn tomorrow.

Give us, Father, such faith in the risen Jesus that we may both trust him for the future life and work wholeheartedly for him in the present. Amen.

Week 8 (Thursday)

1 Corinthians 15:35–41

But someone will ask, 'How are the dead raised? With what kind of body do they come?' Fool! What you sow does not come to life unless it dies. And as for what you sow, you do not sow the body that is to be, but a bare seed, perhaps of wheat or of some other grain. But God gives it a body as he has chosen, and to each kind of seed its own body. Not all flesh is alike, but there is one flesh for human beings, another for animals, another for birds, and another for fish. There are both heavenly bodies and earthly bodies, but the glory of the heavenly is one thing, and that of the earthly is another. There is one glory of the sun, and another glory of the moon, and another glory of the stars; indeed, star differs from star in glory.

Paul now faces the problem that everyone must face if they try to argue through the question of how the resurrection actually works. It's quite easy to talk about life after death if you decide that our future existence will be what we at present call 'disembodied'. It is a lot harder if, with Paul, we believe in the radical goodness of God's creation, and hence in God's ineradicable purpose to renew the embodied state of all his people. We are, in short, at a place where theologians, like physicists, must get used to finding themselves: at the borders of human language. We simply don't have words, and nor did Paul, to describe what the new creation is actually like. All we have is a blueprint, a prototype, in the resurrection of Jesus himself from the dead.

Jesus had not, it appears, merely been 'resuscitated' from the dead. He had not experienced what Lazarus experienced in being brought back from death into the same sort of life as before. As he says in Romans 6:9, Christ was raised once from the dead and will never die again. Death has no more dominion over him, because he has passed on into the new world that death cannot touch. For this reason we find in Paul's words here, and in all the Gospel accounts of Jesus' resurrection, that Jesus' body is both physical and more than physical. We can use a word like 'transphysical', if we wish, but that word, like all such words, is in fact a signpost pointing into a mystery. Such signposts are not without their value. They remind us that the truth will be found down this road, rather than any other, even if at the moment we don't have precise language for what we will find when we get there.

Paul turns to this central question in verse 35, the question of what sort of body the dead will have when they are raised. Resurrection will mean transformation; it will not mean the abandonment of the body, nor will it mean its mere resuscitation. Jesus had spoken in John 12:24 of a grain of wheat falling in the earth, dying, and so bearing much fruit. Paul now uses a very similar image in verse 36. 'What you sow,' he says, 'does not come to life unless it dies.' And you do not sow the body that is to be, but a seed. You don't sow an oak tree, you sow an acorn. You don't sow a daffodil, you sow a daffodil bulb. And God gives to every kind of seed a fitting new body, each to its kind. (v. 38)

As C.S. Lewis recognized in his marvellous book *The Great Divorce*, the life to come is *more* real than the present life, not less. As Paul himself said in a passage we examined a few weeks ago, the desire of the Christian is not to be unclothed, to be left with a disembodied spirit. Our deepest desire is to be more fully clothed, to receive the new body that will live in God's new creation.

He points out in verses 39–41 that even in this life there are different ways of being physical. Not all flesh is alike. There is human flesh, animal flesh, birds' flesh, fishes' flesh. There are both heavenly bodies and earthly bodies (v. 40). The sun, the moon and the stars all have their own peculiarity, their own particular type of existence, and indeed one star differs from another in glory, not just in how it shines, how it looks, but in its very identity. What Paul is doing here is simply pointing out that there are different sorts of physicalities. He is cracking open a simplistic materialism, whether for the Corinthians or for us, that would say that something is either physical or it is not physical. Either it is something that we can touch and see, taste and handle, or it is purely 'spiritual', no more than an idea in someone's mind. This is the first part of the argument that he wants them to grasp, and the very foundation of what he is now going to conclude about the resurrection.

As the seed sown grows into a new form, Father, so grant that our lives may be the seed not only for our future selves but for the great harvest of your kingdom. Amen.

WEEK 8 (FRIDAY)

1 CORINTHIANS 15:42-49

So it is with the resurrection of the dead. What is sown is perishable, what is raised is imperishable. It is sown in dishonour, it is raised in glory. It is sown in weakness, it is raised in power. It is sown a physical body, it is raised a spiritual body. If there is a physical body, there is also a spiritual body. Thus it is written, 'The first man, Adam, became a living being'; the last Adam became a life-giving spirit. But it is not the spiritual that is first, but the physical, and then the spiritual. The first man was from the earth, a man of dust; the second man is from heaven. As was the man of dust, so are those who are of the dust; and as is the man of heaven, so are those who are of heaven. Just as we have borne the image of the man of dust, we will also bear the image of the man of heaven.

Having established that there are different modes of physicality, different ways of being embodied, as we might say, Paul now applies this to the resurrection of the dead. He uses analogies, knowing that they are only partial analogies, but nevertheless, as I said yesterday, that they are also appropriate signposts pointing into the mystery. He uses, first, the signpost of a seed being sown and growing into something new (v. 42). When the body is sown, placed in the ground and buried, it is perishable, part of the present physical order which is subject to decay and to death. When it is raised, as the body of Jesus was raised, it is imperishable. Paul makes the point again that resurrection does not mean returning to the present life, but going through death to the other side, into a life that death will never touch again.

Secondly, in verse 43, he describes the body as sown in dishonour but raised in glory. This is because there is a sense of shame when a body is put into the earth, a sense of sorrow that something good and God-given has gone. Something that was full of life, full of the potential for love and laughter, freedom and joy, has now decayed. But when it is raised, when God gives to this person a new body, they will once again be all that they were, but, so to speak, even more so. They will be full of the love of God, full of the breath of God, full of the new life of God, and they will never lose it. They will be truly what God made them to be. In other words, they will be full of glory, the glory of being a genuine human being made in God's image.

Thirdly, Paul states that the body is sown in weakness, but raised in power. In this present life, there is only so much that we can do and then we fall short. And as we grow older, we are less able to do even the little we can. Ultimately death is the end of that road of weakness. When we are raised, however, we will be raised in power, raised with the ability to do and be all that God intends for us as human beings.

Now follows the verse that has given people so much trouble and has been so often misunderstood. In many translations verse 44 states: 'It is sown a physical body, it is raised a spiritual body.' In our culture the split between physical and spiritual is almost invariably made in a way that goes back to the philosopher Plato. He presented the physical world as being a secondary, shabby and rather evil sort of place. In striking contrast, he thought of the world of forms or of spirits as a non-physical place, a superior reality which had left behind entirely the constraints of space, time and matter. Paul, however, is very clearly not making that contrast; if our Bible translation gives that impression, we should search for a better one if possible—although, as I said earlier, theologians are here of course at the borders of language.

The word Paul uses for 'physical' in the phrase 'it is sown a physical body' is a word that really means 'that which is animated by soul'. This present body is animated by the ordinary human personality, the soul or heart of a person. The new body, promised after resurrection, will be animated by God's spirit. It will be 'spiritual', not in the sense of 'non-physical', but in the sense that God's spirit will provide its life. Throughout his theology (for instance in Romans 8:9–11) Paul sees the Spirit of God as the means by which God raised Jesus from the dead, and the means by which God will give us our renewed bodies. These new bodies will be created, breathed into life, by God's own Spirit, God's breath. As Paul says in v. 45: 'The first man, Adam, became a living being;

the last Adam [that is Jesus, the Messiah] became a life-giving spirit.' Jesus, now raised from the dead himself, ascended and glorified, has poured out his own Spirit on his people, and that Spirit will give them new life.

And so, in contrast to what the Corinthians were imagining, they do not yet have the full life that God intends for them. What they have at the moment is the present God-given creation, a body that is animated by the soul. What they will have in the future is a body animated by God's own Spirit. The first man, Adam, was from the earth, a man of dust. The second man is from heaven. The new humanity that God will give comes from God's space, from God's reality, God's mode of being. And in verse 48 we read the good news for all who face death: 'As was the man of dust, so are those who are of the dust; and as is the man from heaven, so are those who are of heaven.' In other words, Jesus now has an existence that comes from God, the gift of God, in which we will all eventually share.

As with the contrast between physical and spiritual, we must remind ourselves that, for Paul, the contrast between earth and heaven is not the contrast between the 'physical' in the sense of space, time and matter, and the 'spiritual' in the sense of non-space, non-time and non-matter. It is the contrast between God's reality and our reality. God's reality is the heavenly reality, and Jesus has already gone into that reality as a human being, clothed in his new body. One day, God will make new heavens and new earth, and marry those two realities together so that there will be one whole, new creation. It will be what we now call 'physical', but somehow more so; and it will be what we now call 'spiritual', but much much more so, because the two realms will be married together.

Coming to verse 49, we reach the climax of what Paul wants to say. Just as we have borne the image of the man of dust, the likeness of Adam, so we will also bear the image of Jesus, the heavenly man. Here Paul deliberately evokes the picture of human beings made in the image of God, as in the first chapter of Genesis. Human beings were made to reflect the image and likeness of God. At the moment we do that only fitfully and partially, because we do not reflect God's image in so far as we decay, grow old and one day die. This decay merely reflects the way the world is, not the way that God is. God intends that one day we shall reflect his image truly: we will be creatures reflecting the very likeness of God as brightly as mirrors. For that we will need new bodies to radiate sufficiently the love, power, joy, grace, freedom, and sheer happiness of God into and throughout his creation.

Thank you, Father, that in his resurrection Jesus has brought into existence the new world that you now invite us to share. Amen.

WEEK 8 (SATURDAY)

1 CORINTHIANS 15:50–58

What I am saying, brothers and sisters, is this: flesh and blood cannot inherit the kingdom of God, nor does the perishable inherit the imperishable. Listen, I will tell you a mystery! We will not all die, but we will all be changed, in a moment, in the twinkling of an eye, at the last trumpet. For the trumpet will sound, and the dead will be raised imperishable, and we will be changed. For this perishable body must put on imperishability, and this mortal body must put on immortality. When this perishable body puts on imperishability, and this mortal body puts on immortality, then the saying that is written will be fulfilled: 'Death has been swallowed up in victory.' 'Where, O death, is your victory? Where, O death, is your sting?' The sting of death is sin, and the power of sin is the law. But thanks be to God, who gives us the victory through our Lord Jesus Christ.

Therefore, my beloved, be steadfast, immovable, always excelling in the work of the Lord, because you know that in the Lord your labour is not in vain.

As so often at the end of a long argument, Paul now draws together the threads of what he is saying in one climactic and triumphant statement. His conclusion is that the present state of human existence cannot be final. What we have at the moment is flesh and blood; this is often misunderstood, like his language about 'physical' and 'spiritual'. People think that by 'flesh and blood' he means what we call 'physical' existence, and therefore that by 'resurrection life' he must mean something different, something 'non-physical'. We must realize that for Paul the word 'flesh' always carries negative connotations. He seldom if ever simply means 'physical'. He uses it to refer to that which is at present decaying, which is rebelling against God; this is what he means when he talks about people being 'in the flesh' or about Jews being Jews 'according to the flesh'. This is precisely the sense in which he uses the word here to express the present way of living and dying which cannot be affirmed as God's final intention for his human creatures. When Paul speaks of blood, this again has particular connotations of racial identity, of family likeness, of blood membership of a people, a family. And that is not how the people of God is formed. They are linked by grace, not by race, because the present state of human existence cannot inherit the kingdom of God (v. 50). However much wonderful spirituality, and intimacy with God, we may enjoy in the present body, it cannot be the body that God intends us ultimately to have.

Therefore Paul looks ahead, pointing to the heart of the mystery (v. 51). There will come a time when we shall not all die, but we shall all be changed. Our present bodies will not be abandoned, as though God disliked physicality and was determined to rid his world of it; they will be transformed. This is what happened to Jesus, and that is what will happen to all Jesus' people. At the last day, when God makes the new heavens and new earth, the body that we have now will be transformed, 'in a moment, in the twinkling of an eye, at the last trumpet' (v. 52). Paul uses here an image drawn from many Jewish texts, appropriate to God's creation of new heavens and a new earth. Paul would have dismissed the idea that he might have meant a real trumpeter. This is wonderful imagery pointing towards the reality that God will create. In whatever way God desires, a great moment will come when all will be changed. The dead, those who have died ahead of this time, will be raised to a life that death cannot touch, while those who are still alive—and Paul envisages the possibility that he might still be alive—will be transformed. The present body is perishable (v. 53), and it must become imperishable. The present body is mortal, heading for death, and it must put on immortality as a new layer. The acorn becomes an oak, the shadow becomes substance. That which we are at the moment— corruptible, decaying, heading for death—will become a new body, full of potential and possibility and new life.

This, then, will be the final fulfilment of all that the prophets had said about death being swallowed up in victory, death losing its sting. Death stings because it reminds us that we have all chosen the way of corruption, the way of decay. We have all gone astray and become idolaters, worshipping the creatures rather than the creator. And Paul knew that the Jews are not only as fragile and frail as the rest of us; they are constantly reminded of the fact by the law, God's good gift to God's people. The law simply and inescapably confirms to them that they are sinful.

In verse 57, however, Paul can rejoice that God has given us the victory through our Lord Jesus Christ. Although death will carry us all off, until the time when Jesus comes again, ultimate victory is ours. The victory that Jesus won on the cross, which was celebrated on the first Easter day, and which we celebrate with our alleluias in this Easter week, will finally be ours when God gives us our new bodies. Paul rounds off this first full exposition of the resurrection of the dead, not by looking ahead to the future life, but by looking clearly and soberly at the present one. Having pointed into the mystery to come, he now wants the Corinthians to look at the next steps that they must take (v. 58): 'Therefore my beloved, be steadfast, immovable, always excelling in the work of the Lord, because you know that in the Lord your labour is not in vain.' When we look into the mystery of what is to come, we see that God has a glorious future for us, a future in which our present existence will be swallowed up in a newly embodied existence.

What we do in the present existence matters. We are not simply oiling the wheels of a machine that will one day fall off the edge of a cliff. We must continue with our work of building for the kingdom of God. It is not a case of 'building the kingdom of God' by our own efforts. Neither our present holiness nor our present acts of justice and mercy will actually bring in the kingdom, here and now, in all its fulness. To assume that would be to tend towards the mistake made by the Corinthians. The great transformation is still to come. But when it does come, the holiness that we now strive to attain, the Christian work we struggle to achieve, the acts of justice and mercy that we try to accomplish, all our deeds of love and goodness, creativity and beauty—all these will be enhanced, transformed in the new world that God is going to make

We have seen that Jesus was raised from the dead; we have seen that we too will be raised from the dead. We look back to Easter and forward to the new heavens and new earth. But our focus is then brought back to the present. Our calling today, throughout this Eastertide, throughout our life as God's Easter people, is to remain steadfast, immovable, always abounding in the work of the Lord. And we know that what we do here and now, in the strength of the Easter Jesus, will not, will never be, in vain.

Give us, Father, such a clear vision of Jesus, and of your future purposes through him for us and for all the world, that we may work for you cheerfully and wholeheartedly all the days of our life. Amen.